WORLD CUP
GREATEST MOMENTS

First published in the UK in 2026 by Dino Books,
an imprint of Bonnier Books UK,
5th Floor, HYLO, 105 Bunhill Row,
London, EC1Y 8LZ
www.bonnierbooks.co.uk

X @UFHbooks
X @footieheroesbks
www.heroesfootball.com
www.bonnierbooks.co.uk

3 5 7 9 10 8 6 4 2

Paperback ISBN: 978-1-78946-941-7
E-book ISBN: 978-1-78946-973-8

The authorised representative in the EEA is Bonnier Books UK (Ireland) Limited.
Registered office address: Block B, The Crescent Building
Northwood, Santry
Dublin 9, D09 C6X8
Ireland
compliance@bonnierbooks.ie

A CIP catalogue record for this book is available from the British Library

Printed and bound in Great Britain by CPI (UK) Ltd, Croydon CR0 4YY

MATT AND TOM OLDFIELD

ULTIMATE FOOTBALL HEROES

WORLD CUP GREATEST MOMENTS

FROM THE PLAYGROUND TO THE PITCH

DINO

ULTIMATE FOOTBALL HEROES

Matt Oldfield is a children's author focusing on the wonderful world of football. His other books include *Unbelievable Football* (winner of the 2020 Children's Sports Book of the Year) and the *Johnny Ball: Football Genius* series. In association with his writing, Matt also delivers writing workshops in schools.

Cover illustration by Dan Leydon.
To learn more about Dan visit danleydon.com
To purchase his artwork visit etsy.com/shop/footynews
Or just follow him on X: @danleydon

To Noah, Nico, Arlo and Lila – and the exciting summer ahead.

TABLE OF CONTENTS

INTRODUCTION 8

CHAPTER 1 – **GEOFF HURST, 1966** 11

CHAPTER 2 – **PELÉ, 1970** 20

CHAPTER 3 – **JOHAN CRUYFF, 1974** 30

CHAPTER 4 – **FRANZ BECKENBAUER, 1974** 39

CHAPTER 5 – **DIEGO MARADONA, 1986** 47

CHAPTER 6 – **ROBERTO BAGGIO, 1994** 56

CHAPTER 7 – **ZINEDINE ZIDANE, 1998** 66

CHAPTER 8 – **RONALDO, 2002** 75

CHAPTER 9 – **FABIO CANNAVARO, 2006** 86

CHAPTER 10 – **ANDRÉS INIESTA, 2010** 95

CHAPTER 11 – **TIM HOWARD, 2014** 104

CHAPTER 12 – **CRISTIANO RONALDO, 2018** 113

CHAPTER 13 – **HARRY KANE, 2018** 122

CHAPTER 14 – **LIONEL MESSI, 2022** 131

CHAPTER 15 – **KYLIAN MBAPPÉ, 2022** 140

QUIZ 150

HOW THE WORLD CUP 2026 WILL WORK 152

TOURNAMENT PLANNER..................................... 153

DRAW YOUR OWN BADGE 169

DESIGN YOUR OWN KIT 170

PLAY LIKE YOUR HEROES 172

INTRODUCTION

The World Cup is one of those events that stays with you. Many of you reading this book will be at the beginning of your World Cup fan adventure, and there's a very good chance that the highs and lows of the 2026 tournament will kick off some lifetime memories.

Our first tournament in my family was the 1994 World Cup – coincidentally, as in 2026, also hosted by the USA, though as a sole host back then. We were living in South Carolina that summer, as part of a fun year abroad with our dad's job, and football was our favourite sport.

So, you can imagine our reaction when we found out that the tournament was coming up that summer, with dozens of games on TV (at times when we would be awake – unlike in the UK where due to time differences, many games were broadcast late at night) and endless opportunities to watch the best footballers on the planet.

It turned out to be an amazing month, with plenty of upsets, unforgettable moments from Romario and Roberto Baggio, a final cameo from Diego Maradona, and much more. Somehow, it all still feels fresh 32 years later – and we're getting ready to watch this summer's action with our own kids!

That's what makes the World Cup special. More than any other football competition, this is where legends are made and dramatic goals are passed from generation to generation. You usually remember where you were for the joy of wins and the agony of losses. Put simply, it's a tournament that never disappoints.

We have no doubt that the 2026 World Cup will continue that trend. How could it not?! Fans across the globe will be treated to farewell outings (probably!) for Lionel Messi and Cristiano Ronaldo, the next chapter for Kylian Mbappé and Lamine Yamal, and an expanded format with more teams than ever.

But before you sit back and enjoy the games, you need to get warmed up, just like the players. That's where we come in, helping you prepare for the 2026 World Cup with a book that travels through the past 60 years of tournament magic, and looks at 15 players who left their mark on the biggest stage. It's an exclusive club, and we could be welcoming some new members in the very near future.

Enjoy the show!

Matt and Tom

CHAPTER 1

GEOFF HURST, 1966 WORLD CUP

Learning from the bench

When Geoff Hurst joined his England teammates for their first practice before the 1966 World Cup, he could never have guessed what lay ahead in the few weeks that followed. His life was about to change in a major way.

He was still one of the newer faces in the squad, having made his debut earlier that year after good form for West Ham. England had Jimmy Greaves and Roger Hunt as their first-choice strikers, so Geoff would be the supersub. He was fine with that. It was just a thrill to be there, sharing the dressing room with legends like Bobby Charlton and Bobby Moore.

As the 1966 hosts, England would get the advantage of loud home crowds, and Geoff could see the excitement on his friends' faces whenever they talked about the tournament.

'It doesn't get much better than this!' he told them. 'I'm afraid to wake up and find out it's all a dream!'

Everyone seemed to be counting down the days until the action began, and World Cup fever was sweeping across the country.

'This is our year!' one of his neighbours told him every morning.

Geoff smiled and waved. Would he have to move if England were eliminated early?!

Thankfully, they sailed through the group stage with two wins and a draw, and the buzz around the country became deafening. The England team seemed like real contenders, and stadiums were sold out in no time while fans were scrambling to get their hands on tickets.

Geoff tried to make the most of the experience and learn more about international football. That meant he was often glued to the action from his view on the bench. In the match against France, he was so focused on watching the game that he forgot he wasn't just there as a fan. Luckily, one of the other subs nudged him in the ribs and reminded him to go for a warm-up jog on the touchline.

But things could change so fast in the unpredictable football world. By the time England walked out for their next game, Geoff wasn't on the bench with the substitutes anymore. He was on the pitch!

A chance to shine.

Alf Ramsey, the England manager, always reminded Geoff to stay ready – and those words looked even wiser when Jimmy Greaves was ruled out of the quarter-final against Argentina with a leg injury.

'That means you're starting up front,' Coach Ramsey explained, giving Geoff a pat on the back. 'You wouldn't be here if we didn't believe in you, so get out there and score some goals.'

Geoff's head was spinning so fast that he could barely put together a sentence to reply. But his big grin said it all. It wouldn't be an easy task to replace Greaves, but what an opportunity!

'I'm playing in a World Cup quarter-final,' he repeated to himself, trying to get used to the idea of it, while he walked over to the training pitch. This was turning into the wildest year of his life!

But there was no time to doubt himself. He had a job to do. England were playing Argentina, and he knew it would be a tight, physical battle. Without Greaves in the goalscorer role, the fans seemed a little more nervous than usual and were praying that another hero would step forward.

Geoff wanted that kind of responsibility, and he stayed alert as England attacked. He might only get one scoring chance in the whole game, so he had to be ready to take it. When Martin Peters, his West Ham teammate, supplied a cross, Geoff had already darted into the box. He knew where he needed to be. Shaking off his marker, he headed the ball past the keeper.

Gooooooooooooooooooooooaaaaaaaaaaaaaaaaaaaaaallllllllllllllllllllllllllllllllll!!!!!!!!!!!!!!!!!!!!!

'What a header!' Martin called, but it was hard to hear him over the noise in the stadium.

The two players' West Ham connection made all the difference. Geoff had seen Martin whip in hundreds of crosses – in training and in matches – and together they had unlocked the Argentina defence.

That goal was enough to send England through, and Geoff soaked up the congratulations from his teammates in the dressing room.

'Not bad for a West Ham player!' joked Greaves, a proud Tottenham man.

When Bobby Charlton scored twice to clinch a win in the semi-final, it was impossible not to imagine the scenes in London if England lifted the trophy. Geoff was fired up just thinking about it.

With the World Cup final only a few days away, the one big question for Coach Ramsey was whether to go back to Greaves, who had recovered from his injury, or stick with Geoff in the starting 11. The safe choice would have been Greaves, a proven goalscorer for years, but Coach Ramsey trusted what he had seen in the last two games, and Geoff would keep his place for the biggest match in the country's history.

'They think it's all over... it is now!'

Gazing up into the stands, Geoff could hardly believe how many fans had squeezed into Wembley for the final against West Germany. They all wanted to be able to say they were there when England lifted the trophy – but there was a lot of work ahead before the players could think about that.

The stadium went silent when West Germany took an early lead. But England regrouped and shook off the nerves. Geoff was only 24, but he was surrounded by experienced leaders – and they all simply switched into fightback mode.

In no time, the two teams were level – thanks to Geoff. He was at his best when he was making runs in the box, and he proved it again by arriving completely unmarked to head in Bobby Moore's free kick.

Gooooooooooooooooooooooooaaaaaaaaaaaaaaaaaa aaaaallllllllllllllllllllllllllllll!!!!!!!!!!!!!!!!!!!!!

His teammates wrapped him in hugs. That goal really settled the nerves and when he looked over to the touchline, Coach Ramsey gave him a nod and a thumbs up. Geoff nodded back. Coach Ramsey had made a brave decision with his team selection, and

Geoff was paying him back.

The game ended 2–2 after 90 minutes, and the teams dragged their aching bodies into extra time.

Coach Ramsey joined his players on the pitch for a quick team talk. 'Dig deep, lads,' he said. 'We just need one chance to win this.'

Geoff got the message, and he still had enough energy to be in the box. When he controlled a cross from the right wing, he saw that the nearest West Germany defender had given him too much space. Big mistake! Geoff fired a quick shot that rattled against the underside of the bar and bounced down near the goal line.

Was it in? England said yes. West Germany said no.

There were no replays to help the referee, so he ran over to the assistant referee for another opinion. Five seconds later, he gave the signal.

Goooooooooooooooooooooooaaaaaaaaaaaaaaaaa aaaaalllllllllllllllllllllllllllllllllll!!!!!!!!!!!!!!!!!!!!!!

It was a shot that would be debated for years, but Geoff didn't care that day. The scoreline said it was a goal, and that was all that counted. He jumped into the air waving his arms, and the England players knew they were close to winning. Now, they just had to defend.

'Get it away!' Coach Ramsey yelled from the touchline while England were trying to clear the ball.

The final whistle was just seconds away when Geoff dribbled up the pitch on a long run. He was mainly just trying to get the ball as far away from the England net as possible. But he was faster than his marker and he raced into the penalty area.

'And here comes Hurst,' the commentator said. 'Some people are on the pitch. They think it's all over…'

Geoff made up his mind to hammer a shot as hard as he could. If it flew over or wide, that was okay; it would use up more precious seconds. But the ball didn't fly over or wide. It flew into the top corner.

'It is now!' the commentator finished.

Goooooooooooooooooooooooaaaaaaaaaaaaaaaaa aaaaalllllllllllllllllllllllllllllll!!!!!!!!!!!!!!!!!!!!!!!

A hat-trick in the World Cup final! It was all of

Geoff's childhood wishes rolled into one. Best of all, England had won the World Cup for the first time. At the final whistle, there were people everywhere – teammates, coaches, fans, police. The joy spread all around Wembley.

Then it was time to walk up the steps, shake his hands with the Queen and get a close-up look at the World Cup trophy. Geoff tried to remember every detail of the occasion. He had a feeling that he was going to be telling stories about this day for a long time!

The England players had become legends that summer, and Geoff's goals had delivered the perfect ending.

CHAPTER 2

PELÉ, 1970 WORLD CUP

One last World Cup ride

Pelé loved the World Cup, and he loved his country. Those were the main reasons that he was about to put on the Brazil shirt again for one final World Cup run. He already had winners' medals from 1958 and 1962, but he had withdrawn from international football after the disappointment of the 1966 tournament, when Brazil failed to make it past group stage.

During the late 1960s, Brazilians were going through hard times. Violence and fear were becoming more common, and the people needed something to bring them together and forget their troubles. The calls for Pelé to boost morale and return to the Brazil team grew louder and louder.

'The 1970 World Cup is just months away and we need Pelé.'

'He's the greatest player the world has ever seen, and we'll win the tournament if he plays.'

'His Brazil career can't end with that horrible 1966 World Cup.'

Pelé gave it a lot of thought, discussed his options with friends and family, and eventually agreed to rejoin the Brazil squad. But could he still dominate like he had in 1958 as a teenager? Did he still have the same talent that had driven Santos, his club in Brazil, to claim trophy after trophy?

The answers to those questions would have to remain a mystery until Pelé and Brazil were on the pitch at Mexico 1970 for their first game, but his teammates were thrilled to have him there.

'We can beat anyone now!' Jairzinho said excitedly. 'The King is back!'

'I wish I was a striker!' defender Carlos Alberto added. 'We're going to be scoring a lot of goals!'

Soon Pelé was putting on his boots for practice and feeling the familiar buzz of playing football for Brazil. He was 29 years old now, but he remained as excited as when he had made his debut. He couldn't wait to remind the world what he could do.

At half-time in the first group game, against Czechoslovakia, Pelé feared he had made the wrong decision. Brazil were drawing 1–1, and looked rusty. Was his comeback a big mistake?

Pelé shook his head. He hadn't got this far by doubting himself, and there was still time to turn things around.

'Forget about the first half,' he told his teammates. 'We're going to be better in the second half.'

He said it with such confidence that the whole dressing room seemed to absorb a spark of energy. If Pelé still believed they could win, they believed it too.

As if he had flipped a switch, Pelé was soon dribbling with his old flair, gliding past defenders and charging towards the goal. No one could get near him. Brazil launched attack after attack, cruising to a 4–1 win.

Maybe they just needed that early test. Once they had their swagger back, the flicks and tricks came out, and Pelé was at the centre of it all. Brazil rolled on with three more victories, setting up a tasty semi-final against Uruguay.

Taking down the rivals

Uruguay had a strong history at the World Cup, winning the first-ever tournament in 1930 and lifting the trophy again in 1950 with a win over Brazil. That had created a bruising rivalry, and now, 20 years on, they were battling it out in the 1970 World Cup semi-final.

When Uruguay took the lead, Pelé didn't panic. If anything, it nudged him into a more ruthless mode. This was his chance to sprinkle a little more Pelé magic on a big game. He called for the ball, shrugged off physical Uruguayan defenders and turned the match in Brazil's favour.

From 1–0 down, Brazil surged into a 3–1 lead, with Pelé helping to set up goals for Jairzinho and Rivellino. Uruguay had planned to mark Pelé tightly, but that plan had been abandoned. He was just too good at finding space, and he dribbled away from defenders before they could get close enough to stop him. The fact that a grinning Pelé seemed to be having the time of his life just added to the Uruguayans' frustration.

Then another through-ball sent Pelé behind the defence and he saw the keeper running off his line towards him. With an outrageous dummy, Pelé let the ball run past the keeper and skipped round to get to it first, but his shot went just wide.

'That would have been the goal of the tournament!' Jairzinho shouted, with a stunned look on his face.

Pelé smiled. Another goal would have been nice, but Brazil could now look forward to the final. He was so close to finishing his farewell World Cup in style.

King Pelé

Pelé couldn't sleep. There were too many thoughts flying through his head. Tomorrow was the World Cup final – Brazil vs Italy – and it might just be the biggest day of his life. Fans across the globe would be watching, and millions of Brazilians would be counting on him to deliver another trophy. Yes, that kind of pressure and excitement was keeping him awake.

Pelé finally drifted off to sleep and woke up in the morning with a burst of energy and determination flowing through his body. He took a deep breath and opened the curtains to let in the morning sunshine.

'It looks like the perfect day to win a World Cup,' he said to himself, smiling.

He would always remember the bus journey to the Azteca Stadium on that day of the final. Looking out of the window, he saw Brazil flags everywhere – a sea of yellow and green. Feeling the love from the fans but also feeling the sadness of playing in his last World Cup game, tears trickled down Pelé's cheeks.

Walking into the dressing room, he tried to replace the tears with a calming grin, and he shook hands with Rivellino and Jairzinho, who had been alongside him through all the battles at this tournament.

'We're following your lead, King,' Rivellino said, patting Pelé on the shoulder. 'Let's bring this trophy home.'

'Don't worry, we're going to make this the perfect ending,' Jairzinho added. 'That's what you deserve.'

'You guys are the best,' Pelé replied, his voice choking up with emotion.

The roar of the crowd gave Pelé goosebumps when the teams walked onto the pitch, and he carried that feeling into the match.

A Brazil throw-in dropped to Rivellino, but an Italy defender rushed towards him. Rivellino just had time to loop a hopeful cross into the box, and Pelé instantly saw where it was going to land. He took a few quick steps towards the back post and jumped as high as he could while keeping both eyes on the ball. He got up higher than his marker and thumped a powerful downward header past the Italy goalkeeper and into the bottom corner.

Gooooooooooooooooooooooooaaaaaaaaaaaaaaaaaaaaaallllllllllllllllllllllllllllllllllll!!!!!!!!!!!!!!!!!!!!

Pelé was on the ground, but looking up, he could see the ball in the back of the net. Making his way back to the halfway line he felt as though he was walking on air. What a feeling!

A defensive mistake gifted Italy an equaliser, and suddenly it was 1–1.

'It's okay!' Pelé called, reassuring the nervous faces among his team's defenders, and encouraging them with the words: 'We'll get another goal.'

Brazil pushed forward again. Pelé went close with a chance at the back post, then Gérson thumped a shot into the net from the edge of the penalty area. 2–1.

When Gérson floated the ball over the Italian defence, Pelé was a step ahead. Out of the corner of his eye, he could see Jairzinho sprinting into the box, and he cushioned a header towards him. Jairzinho was almost running too fast and he scuffed his shot a little, but it was enough to wrong-foot the goalkeeper. The ball trickled into the net. 3–1.

The perfect goodbye

Pelé could see some of the Italy players holding their heads or hunched over with their hands on their knees. It was a long way back for them now. He knew that Brazil just had to let the minutes tick away.

They moved forward from the back again, passing

down the left wing. Jairzinho collected a long pass, cut inside and laid the ball off to Pelé. Again, Pelé knew exactly what he wanted to do even before the ball reached him. He could sense Carlos Alberto racing forward from right-back and he calmly rolled a pass to him. It was the perfect speed – not too fast, not too slow – and Carlos Alberto hit his shot the first time, arrowing it into the bottom corner. 4–1.

Now the party could really start!

At the final whistle, fans poured onto the pitch. Before he even had a chance to raise his arms in celebration, Pelé was surrounded by fans, teammates and even a few of the Italy players. People congratulated him with hugs and handshakes, and some wanted his shirt, his shorts and his boots. His shirt was the first to go, and then his teammates lifted him onto their shoulders and carried him on a lap of the stadium. They all knew what it meant to him to be on top of the world again.

At last, after an eight-year gap, Pelé had the World Cup trophy in his hands again. He just stared at it, with the biggest smile on his face.

'I've missed you!' he said quietly.

He had previously allowed himself to imagine this moment, to be reunited with the greatest prize of all, but none of that came close to the pride and happiness he really felt now.

The football world had begged for one more special Pelé tournament – and he had delivered. The crowd was chanting his name again, with Brazil flags everywhere, and he knew he was leaving behind a really special World Cup legacy.

'Pelé! Pelé! Pelé!'

CHAPTER 3

JOHAN CRUYFF, 1974 WORLD CUP

Total Football

Brazil had won three of the last four World Cups with their breathtaking attacking play. But Pelé had retired from international football, and so there was a gap for a new entertainer. Enter Johan Cruyff, the Dutch maestro.

Johan and Coach Rinus Michels had built a Total Football approach during their time together at Ajax, and now they were reuniting with the Netherlands national team. It seemed like a safe guess that this combination would lead to some incredible highlights.

The Total Football philosophy allowed attackers to

feel free in drifting around the pitch, so that players could use their instincts to create passing moves that baffled defences. Johan was at the heart of this philosophy, and his creative brain was what really made Total Football work.

Even better, Johan was in his prime. He had won the Ballon d'Or in 1971 and 1973, and he had fired Ajax to three straight European Cups with dribbling runs and vital goals. The 1974 World Cup was coming at the ideal moment.

'This is our time,' he told his teammates. 'These other countries are about to see what Total Football is all about.'

International success was one of the last missing pieces in Johan's football career, and he knew the Netherlands had a real chance of lifting the trophy this time.

The 1974 World Cup in West Germany mattered even more to Johan because he had missed the World Cup four years earlier. He was determined to make up for lost time, and now it was up to him to leave his mark on the tournament.

'The Cruyff Turn'

Tickets had sold out, and the stadium was packed out, with a crowd eager to see the Netherlands' group game against Sweden. In truth, most of those fans had come to see one man: Johan.

Walking onto the pitch with his teammates, Johan showed no hint of nerves. Instead, he strolled on with the confidence of a man who had repeatedly won the biggest games in his career. Pressure? What pressure?

When the Netherlands won possession, Johan drifted over to the left wing, as he liked to do. The Total Football style of play made that simple, and the Swedish defenders tried to work out who would follow him.

For once, only one marker went with him – right back Jan Olsson. Johan's eyes lit up as a long pass arrowed towards him and he saw that he would have space to take the defender on. He cushioned the ball with his right foot, and then instinct took over.

Johan faked to cross the ball into the box straightaway and sensed Olsson falling for the trick. It was understandable in a way. Johan had fired in early crosses twice already during the first half.

But this time, he had a different plan. As Olsson got ready to block the cross, Johan dragged the ball back with the inside of his right foot, sending it slightly behind him. In one movement, he turned back in the opposite direction and sprinted into the box. *See ya!*

The crowd responded with oohs and aahs, then a small groan as the cross was scrambled away. But there was even more noise around the stadium whenever Johan got the ball. The fans inched towards the edge of their seats, and the Sweden defenders looked like they had seen a ghost.

At half-time, Johan's teammates were still bubbling with excitement about his performance and trying to understand how he had done it.

'There's no way I'd even attempt that!' one of the Dutch defenders said. 'I'd trip myself up without even touching the ball, and I'd prefer not to do that in front of thousands of people.'

Despite all the Netherlands' attacks, the match finished 0–0, but Johan's magical moment dominated all post-match conversation. No one had seen that move before. They all called it 'The Cruyff Turn'.

'Was that something he had practised?'

'Where had he learned it?'

'What made him use that skill today?'

'Had he been saving it for the World Cup?'

Johan grinned at all the questions from the reporters. The answers were quite simple. He had never seen it done and had never practised it. It was all pure football genius.

'It just sort of happened!' he said, smiling and shrugging.

That just added to the mystery, and the reporters only had more questions.

Johan joined his teammates on the bus just outside the stadium. He had a feeling that many other players would soon be working on that move, too. But he could never have guessed that it would live on as an essential skill for 50 years and counting.

On target

As the second group stage of the 1974 World Cup started, Johan was still looking for his first goal of the tournament, but he wouldn't have to wait much longer. Against Argentina, he was on the move as soon as the Netherlands won the ball back. He timed his run perfectly, and the defenders looked desperately for an offside flag.

There was no one around him, but Johan still had to control the floated pass. He watched the ball carefully, cushioned it with his right foot and dodged the Argentina keeper, who came flying off his line.

'Don't fall! Don't fall!' Johan told himself, while trying to keep his balance. He stumbled a little but still had time to poke the ball into the empty net.

Gooooooooooooooooooooooooaaaaaaaaaaaaaaaaaa aaaaallllllllllllllllllllllllllllllll!!!!!!!!!!!!!!!!!!!!!!

Next, he popped up on the left wing, dribbled forward and whipped in a brilliant cross to help create another goal with Rep.

He wasn't done yet, though. In the 90th minute of the game, with the Netherlands 3–0 up, he was lurking when a rebound dropped towards the edge of the box. Without even needing a first touch to control the ball, he arrowed a shot into the bottom corner.

Gooooooooooooooooooooooaaaaaaaaaaaaaaaaa aaaaallllllllllllllllllllllllllllllll!!!!!!!!!!!!!!!!!!!!

It was total domination, and Johan could hear the Dutch fans singing in the crowd. They were all starting to believe that the team was on the road to glory. One thing was clear: no other country was playing at the level of the Netherlands.

In the semi-final, they just had to beat Brazil, the defending World Cup champions, to clinch a place in the final. Once again, Johan was the difference-maker. He escaped down the right wing and clipped a pass through to Neeskens, another Dutch attacker with the first name of Johan, who floated a shot over the keeper. 1–0!

More gaps appeared and the Netherlands attacked down the left wing. Johan sensed a chance and sprinted up in support. The cross flew into the box, and he steered a thumping first-time shot into the net.

Gooooooooooooooooooooooaaaaaaaaaaaaaaaaa aaaaallllllllllllllllllllllllllllllll!!!!!!!!!!!!!!!!!!!!

'World Cup final, here we come!' Johan shouted,

punching the air and thinking about all the fans back home watching the game.

The final test.

'This is our chance to be heroes forever with one more special performance!' Johan said. In the dressing room, before the final against the host nation, West Germany, it was growing quieter. All the Dutch players were having similar thoughts and trying to keep their nerves under control. Some of them had played in European finals before, but they understood that winning the World Cup for their country was an even bigger deal.

Johan felt the hairs on the back of his neck standing up during the airing of the Dutch national anthem, and memories from his football journey came flooding into his mind. He had dreamed about this kind of occasion since he was a little boy, and now he was standing here in that famous orange shirt, with the World Cup trophy within reach.

'Let's go!!!' he yelled, stepping forward for the kick-off. The whistle blew and he passed the ball back to Neeskens. Game on!

That simple pass turned out to be the start of a sweeping attack. The Netherlands moved the ball around the pitch with 15 passes straight from the kick-off, before Johan surged forward. A West German tackle was a second too late, tripping him in the box. Penalty!

'West Germany haven't even touched the ball yet!' Johan thought, while watching Neeskens step forward for the penalty.

Neeskens made no mistake, scoring the penalty and stunning the home crowd. Just for a minute, Johan soaked it all in. The Netherlands were ahead in the World Cup final!

But little by little, the game slipped away. West Germany turned the game around to take a 2–1 lead, and Johan was so tightly marked that on this occasion, he couldn't drag the Netherlands back into the match.

The West Germany players hugged and waved to the cheering crowd at the final whistle, but Johan had a sick feeling in his stomach. He would bounce back, but this loss was going to sting for a long time.

CHAPTER 4

FRANZ BECKENBAUER, 1974 WORLD CUP

Changing the game

While the football world was being wowed by the Netherlands, Franz Beckenbauer was busily working hard on his own aims. Put simply, by the summer of 1974, Franz was a winner. He had led a dominant Bayern Munich to three German titles in a row, plus the latest European Cup, and he already had a Ballon d'Or trophy as part of his collection.

But he still walked onto the pitch at the 1974 World Cup with something to prove. This was Franz's third World Cup, and the past two had ended in heartbreak for him and his national team.

West Germany had to get it right this time. They

had flexed their muscles by winning the 1972 European Championships, and now the World Cup was in their sights.

Franz, the man known as 'Der Kaiser' ('The Emperor') had started his career as a midfielder before switching into a position that was new in the football world – the sweeper role. That meant dropping deeper behind the defence, but it gave him the freedom to bring the ball forward. Week after week, Franz controlled games at both ends of the pitch.

As a sweeper, he could use all of his strengths, from his passing and vision to his positioning and tackling. He was so good at it that other teams started to experiment with the position, too.

With Franz running the show, West Germany set off on their path towards World Cup glory, beating Chile and Australia. They were even better in the second group stage, winning all three games, keeping two more clean sheets and clinching their place in the final.

'We've got a great chance if we keep playing like this,' Franz told teammates Gerd Müller and Paul Breitner.

Gerd and Paul nodded. They had been banging in the goals, but they both knew that Franz was the engine of the team.

'It all starts with you, Kaiser,' Gerd said. 'We're going to need you even more in the final.'

Franz smiled. He had already been thinking about the final, where West Germany would face Johan Cruyff and the Netherlands, and he had some ideas on how to turn the game in their favour.

Following the game plan (eventually)

'If Johan gets the ball here, we've got to be closer,' Franz explained, pointing to the tactics board in the dressing room. 'We need to make him feel like he's crowded at all times.'

It had been two days since West Germany had clinched their place in the 1974 World Cup final, beating Poland in the decisive group game, and most of that time had been spent on a game plan for stopping the Netherlands.

Franz loved to get into the details, and the rest of the West German defenders were huddled around him as he added his thoughts to the coaches' instructions. Everyone in the room could tell that he would go on to be a manager himself one day.

'It's going to take a team effort,' he added. 'We've got to stay connected.'

All these conversations helped Franz brush aside any fears that he might leave another World Cup empty-handed. West Germany had lost the 1966 World Cup final against England in extra time, then finished third in the 1970 World Cup. He was tired of seeing other teams celebrate with the trophy.

The 1974 final started disastrously for the Germans. The Netherlands raced forward and scored in the second minute.

Franz stood with his hands on his hips. Were West Germany still asleep?! But as captain, he couldn't let this early disappointment unsettle his teammates, so he refocused on the game plan. Everything they had prepared was still key. It would be their route back into the match.

Franz won tackles, intercepted passes and sparked his team into life. Paul equalised with a penalty, then

Gerd put the West Germans ahead. The momentum had completely shifted, and the fans were cheering every pass.

'Don't stop running now!' Franz called to his teammates. He was sticking close to Johan and stopping Dutch attacks before they went anywhere.

West Germany were closing in on the big prize, and Franz was in the zone.

Paving the way for future champions

Some players faded as the game went on, but Franz got stronger. He could feel that West Germany were on top, and he refused to let the Netherlands back into the game.

This was the value of Franz's sweeper role. He could decide to limit his surging runs forward from defence and focus instead on giving instructions to the players in front of him.

'Drop back and watch the bounce!'

'Follow that run!'

'Don't give him any space!'

The Dutch players were getting more and more

frustrated as they ran out of time, and Franz always seemed to be in their way when they got close to the German net. Like a mind-reader, he predicted where through balls would go, and he stayed a step ahead of the chasing strikers. It was a masterclass in how to defend a lead.

At last, Franz heard the final whistle, and it all started to sink in. Third time lucky! He was a World Cup winner, and it was extra special to do it in front of his home fans.

There was something new for West Germany at the presentation ceremony, too. After winning the previous World Cup, the Brazilians had been allowed to keep the trophy as the first team to lift it three times, and a decision was made to create a new trophy. West Germany were the first country to win it – and it was the famous trophy that would be passed on for decades to come.

Franz held it tightly in two hands, just to make sure he didn't drop it.

'It was worth the wait!' he said, smiling. 'What a trophy!'

As the years passed, Franz's impact went far beyond that famous night in 1974. His mentality was passed on to future German national squads, helping to form the identity of a professional, organised team that always had a chance at major tournaments.

'We didn't invent magical football or the beautiful game,' Franz would later explain. 'Germans have to work to achieve their success.'

In fact, Franz was able to apply some of those philosophies directly. He took over as the manager of West Germany in 1984 and guided his country to back-to-back World Cup finals, including the 1990 tournament, where they beat Argentina in the final. It didn't quite compare to his playing days, but he loved the challenge of international football.

There had been ups and downs, but by Italia 1990, Franz's relationship with the World Cup had spanned 28 years, and he believed that he had paved the way for his country to stay on top. The Germans would go on to win the European

Championships in 1996 and the World Cup in 2014.

As a player or a manager, when the game was on the line, 'Der Kaiser' was someone you wanted on your side.

CHAPTER 5

DIEGO MARADONA, 1986 WORLD CUP

Born with a gift

Football had always been easy for Diego Maradona. His youth coaches could tell that he had a special gift from his earliest practices. They had never seen anyone move as naturally as Diego with a ball at his feet.

From there, life became a whirlwind. Diego made his Argentina debut as a 16-year-old, and his obvious talent had taken him from Boca Juniors to Barcelona to Napoli by the time he travelled to Mexico for the 1986 World Cup.

Diego was Argentina's most talented player, but his personality was just as important for the team's morale in the dressing room. He went into every game with a fearless intensity, and the rest of the team followed loyally behind him.

He could do things on the pitch that left his teammates stunned. Sure, he was small, but he was also tough and surprisingly hard to knock off the ball. His low centre of gravity meant he could weave in and out of tackles without losing his balance, and he needed to be agile against punishing defenders who targeted his legs.

His first World Cup experience, Spain 1982, had been disappointing. On the pitch, Argentina struggled. Off the pitch, the dressing room was divided, between the older generation, led by the captain Daniel Passarella, and the bold new generation, led by Diego. But in Mexico, there could be no argument about the team's true superstar. Diego was on the form of his life, and he would have to provide the inspiration if Argentina were going to lift the trophy. He was the team's captain now too, and he felt so proud every time he thought about wearing the armband.

'We've got to be ready to do whatever it takes to

win,' he told his teammates before the tournament in Mexico kicked off. 'Are you with me?'

His teammates cheered. They knew he could be fiery at times, but they were all drawn to his aura.

'The Hand of God'

The next test was a quarter-final against England, a country that had become one of Argentina's fiercest rivals. Diego knew his teammates would be ready for the battle, and he was determined to set the tone.

Whenever Diego had the ball, the England players were drawn to him like a magnet. But he trusted his dribbling with even the smallest gaps. On one attack, he effortlessly darted between two midfielders, and then poked a pass to a teammate, who couldn't quite control it.

But a mis-hit England clearance looped backwards into the penalty area. Diego was already on the move, and he reacted fastest to sprint after it. At first, it seemed like it would be an easy catch for the keeper, who was much taller, but Diego jumped as high as he could. At the last second, he twisted his body and used his hand to punch the ball away. It bounced down and into the net.

Surely a handball? But no! The referee gave the signal for a goal.

The England players couldn't believe it. They surrounded the ref, pointing to their hands and yelling, and they pleaded with the assistant referee to disallow it. On the touchline, the England coaches were just as angry.

By now, Diego was already celebrating with his teammates. Had he really got away with it?!

He would later admit what the replays clearly showed. 'It was a little with the head of Maradona and a little with the hand of God,' he explained with a cheeky smile. From that point onwards, the goal would always be known as 'The Hand of God'.

England's protests were dismissed, and Argentina had a 1–0 lead.

Solo magic

That goal left England fuming, and a lot of that anger was directed at Diego. Some players might have tried to stay out of the action for a few minutes to let tempers cool, but not Argentina's little Number 10. He didn't back down from anything or anyone.

'You'll have to catch me first!' Diego thought to himself, calling for the ball.

He dropped back into his own half and received a pass with two players marking him. No problem! His touch didn't let him down, and it seemed like the ball was glued to his foot as he wriggled free from an impossible trap. His feet were too fast for the England midfielders, and once he got moving, there was no chance of them catching him.

Diego saw lots of green grass in front of him, and he dribbled on, cutting between two tacklers, and gliding towards the edge of the box. Somehow, he was getting faster. He leaned to his right to race past another defender as the oohs of the crowd got louder. Now he was in the box and still travelling at electric speed.

The keeper slid out, but Diego danced around him, too, and tucked the ball into the empty net before England could recover.

Gooooooooooooooooooooooaaaaaaaaaaaaaaaaa aaaaallllllllllllllllllllllllllllllllll!!!!!!!!!!!!!!!!!!!!

Wow! Diego heard the cheers while jogging towards the corner flag. He jumped in the air, and his teammates hurried to catch up with him.

England had no complaints about this goal. It was one of the all-time great World Cup goals, and it would be on TV again and again over the years.

'You're a genius!' shouted defender Oscar Ruggeri. 'You just dribbled past their whole team!'

Diego grinned. 'Yeah, I don't think they like me very much right now!' he replied.

Even by Diego's own high standards, it was a stunning goal. He had arrived at the tournament with a big reputation, and he was living up to the hype.

Legends for life

But Diego didn't want a spectacular goal to be his highlight of this World Cup. Argentina were setting their sights much higher than that. In their semi-final against Belgium, Diego was the match-winner again. With a performance packed full of stunning skills and cheeky touches, he carried his team to victory.

When a cross came in from the right wing, Diego darted towards the near post in front of a defender and guided the ball into the net with the outside of his left foot.

Gooooooooooooooooooooooaaaaaaaaaaaaaaaaaaaaaalllllllllllllllllllllllllllllllllll!!!!!!!!!!!!!!!!!!!!!!

It was a beautiful touch – and one that only a magician like Diego could have produced at such a key moment. No one could have done it better.

Another dribbling run put Belgian defenders on the ground as he twisted one way, then the other. He burst into the penalty area before rocketing a shot past the keeper.

Gooooooooooooooooooooooaaaaaaaaaaaaaaaaaaaaaalllllllllllllllllllllllllllllllllll!!!!!!!!!!!!!!!!!!!!!!

Diego didn't even stop as the ball hit the net. He just spun away towards the corner flag. These wonder goals were becoming a regular thing.

'Every game, you do something even more amazing!' Oscar said, wrapping him in a big hug after the game.

Now Diego and Argentina were one game away from capping off an incredible World Cup run – and he understood what this meant. If Argentina beat West Germany in the final, they would be legends for life. If they lost, it might haunt him for the rest of his career.

'We'd better win then!' he said when his teammates talked about those wildly different outcomes.

Diego could feel the emotions bubbling up while he waited impatiently for the kick-off. He desperately wanted to score another magical goal, but he quickly saw that it was going to be hard to repeat his solo heroics. Two German players followed him everywhere, and there was usually a third defender lurking nearby, too.

'I must be really popular!' he joked.

Argentina took a 2–0 lead, but West Germany hit back with two late goals, leaving Diego wondering if he was heading for a cruel end to this tournament.

The next goal would surely win it, and Diego forgot about all his bumps and bruises when he saw midfielder Jorge Burruchaga breaking free ahead of him. He just had to get the ball to him. Diego used all the power he had left to guide a pass forward, and Jorge fired a shot past the keeper.

'Yes!!!!' Diego screamed. A second ago, he could hardly move. Now, he was sprinting to celebrate.

There were just six minutes left. Surely that was it. Diego chased back and helped his defence, then fell to the ground when he heard the sweet sound of the final whistle. Argentina had done it!

With a huge smile, Diego walked forward to collect his medal. He was handed the World Cup trophy and, with his teammates around him, he raised it for everyone to see.

Diego would follow up this success with a stunning season for Napoli in Serie A, but nothing could top what he had done for his country. At the 1986 World Cup, he won the hearts of the people of Argentina, and it was a bond that could never be broken.

CHAPTER 6

ROBERTO BAGGIO, 1994 WORLD CUP

'The Divine Ponytail'

All eyes were on Roberto Baggio, the reigning Ballon d'Or winner, when the Italy squad stepped off the plane in the USA for the 1994 World Cup. Roberto was no stranger to all this attention, and the man known as 'The Divine Ponytail' – for his football miracles and his unique hairstyle – posed for photos. He had dazzled for Juventus in Serie A, but he was about to get a much, much bigger audience.

Everyone knew what to expect from Italy's defence coming into this tournament. They had the brilliant duo of Franco Baresi and Paolo Maldini to shut down star attackers, but could they score enough goals? Even though Roberto had shown he could lead the way with his creative spark, there were question marks surrounding the rest of their attacking approach.

The fears were confirmed when the Italians lost 1–0 to the Republic of Ireland in their opening game. It was the kind of shock that the World Cup could serve up from time to time, but predictably that meant panic and meltdowns back in Italy. No one was safe from the newspaper reporters' criticisms.

Training was tense, as were team meetings, and the Italy players looked like they might fall apart in the scorching American sun. But they limped through to the knockout rounds, finishing third in the group and going through on goal difference. Roberto knew they were very lucky to still be in the tournament.

'We have to be better,' he told his teammates. 'It's been a bad start, but the story isn't over yet. The next round is a new opportunity, and we're going to make the most of it.'

Roberto did just that. With Italy losing 1–0 to

Nigeria, he was the coolest man in the stadium as he steered an inch-perfect shot into the bottom corner for a late equaliser.

Goooooooooooooooooooooooaaaaaaaaaaaaaaaaaaaaaallllllllllllllllllllllllllllllllll!!!!!!!!!!!!!!!!!!!!

Even under the most intense pressure, Roberto had refused to be rattled. He ran towards the fans, and he could see his teammates had the same relieved looks on their faces when they caught up with him.

'We're not done yet!' Roberto yelled. Suddenly, they all believed again. That one goal had changed everything.

When Italy won a penalty in extra time, they turned to their main man again. Roberto took a deep breath, then fired the ball into the bottom corner.

Goooooooooooooooooooooooaaaaaaaaaaaaaaaaaaaaaallllllllllllllllllllllllllllllllll!!!!!!!!!!!!!!!!!!!!

'Don't let us get on a roll!' he joked while he celebrated the win on the pitch with Paolo Maldini and Alessandro Costacurta. 'We're coming for the trophy now!'

At the top of his game

But things could never be simple for Italy. Even with a happier mood, both in training and around the team hotel, the performances on the pitch were like being on one long rollercoaster.

The games started to have a familiar pattern, too. Italy would dig themselves a hole, and Roberto had to dig them back out. With the team wobbling in their quarter-final game against Spain, 'The Divine Ponytail' came to the rescue yet again.

The teams were locked at 1–1 and the match seemed to be heading for extra time. But Roberto had other ideas. Racing onto a chipped pass, he got to the ball first, knocked it round the keeper and drilled a shot from a tight angle. It whistled past the defender on the line and into the net.

Gooooooooooooooooooooooaaaaaaaaaaaaaaaaaaaaaallllllllllllllllllllllllllllll!!!!!!!!!!!!!!!!!!!!

'It's that man again!' the commentator shouted. 'Wow!'

After all the doubts and criticism early in the tournament, Italy were 90 minutes away from the

1994 World Cup final – and Roberto was getting better and better.

He wasn't the only superstar grabbing the headlines, however. Romario was scoring great goals for Brazil, Tomas Brolin was putting Sweden among the contenders, and then there was the team from Bulgaria, who had already taken down some giants, including a strong German squad.

The Bulgarians now had Italy in their sights. But before they could think about another upset, Roberto slammed the door shut. It wasn't as if Bulgaria didn't know he was the danger man. They swarmed around him every time he got the ball, but then they switched off for two costly seconds.

Roberto got free from a throw-in, spun away from his marker, then danced past another defender with a drop of the shoulder. From the edge of the box, he curled a shot into the far corner.

Gooooooooooooooooooooooaaaaaaaaaaaaaaaaa aaaaalllllllllllllllllllllllllllllllll!!!!!!!!!!!!!!!!!!!!!!

It all happened in a flash. Bulgaria were stunned, but the Italy fans were in dreamland.

A few minutes later, Roberto was celebrating again after another deadly finish. He made a clever run behind the defence and knew there was a chance for a shot. Some players might have thought about a cross to set up a teammate. In fact, on other days, Roberto might have done that. But he was on the form of his life, so he just decided to swing his foot at it.

Before anyone could react, he thumped a rocket strike across the Bulgaria keeper. He couldn't have hit it any better, and he swivelled just in time to see the ball fly into the bottom corner.

Gooooooooooooooooooooooooaaaaaaaaaaaaaaaaaaaaaaallllllllllllllllllllllllllllllllll!!!!!!!!!!!!!!!!!!!!!!!

'Just so you know, I expect you to score every time you get the ball now,' Paolo said, laughing. 'Maybe you could try scoring direct from a corner next!'

But the game took a tough turn for Italy in the second half. Bulgaria had already pulled a goal back, and then Roberto felt a sharp pain in his hamstring as he ran forward. He instantly knew it was bad news and signalled to the bench for a substitution. Uh-oh!

Italy survived the final 20 minutes, but that was

only part of the equation now. Roberto's injury quickly became the biggest storyline as the Italians prepared to take on Brazil in the final. He just hoped that he would be on the pitch with his teammates.

A cruel twist

'I'll do whatever it takes,' Roberto explained to the doctors and physios. 'Please. I can't miss the final.'

They came up with a plan, but there was no simple cure for a hamstring injury. Normally, the suggestion would have been a few weeks of rest. Instead, they had only a few days to work on his treatment.

It just seemed so unfair. After all the hard work and special goals, there was no chance of Roberto being 100 per cent fit for the biggest game of his life. But he knew he had to try – and his coaches agreed that he had earned that right. Italy would never have reached the World Cup final without his magic moments.

As the kick-off for the final loomed, Roberto knew which movements were pain free and which movements made the injury worse. After a gentle warm-up, he sat quietly in the dressing room and tried to picture the game in his mind. He wouldn't be making runs behind the defence as often, but his football brain could still take over.

Then it was showtime. He walked down the tunnel and stood next to his teammates for the national anthem, praying that the electric buzz of a World Cup final would get him through the match.

With his hamstring bandaged, Roberto did the best he could. There was nothing wrong with his touch and technique, and he soon had the Brazil defenders scrambling. Somehow, he battled his way through the whole game, including the 30 minutes of extra time, and was still standing as the 0–0 stalemate headed for penalties.

'That was heroic, man,' Paolo said to Roberto, putting an arm round his shoulders. 'You did everything you could.'

Roberto gave him a tired smile and nodded. But he still had one last task ahead.

Coach Sacchi gave Roberto the fifth penalty in the shoot-out, but Italy had already missed twice by the time it was his turn. He walked forward slowly, like a man with the whole world weighing on his shoulders. If he missed, Italy's dream was over.

Nothing could match the pressure of a World Cup final, but Roberto had taken penalties in big matches before and he wanted this responsibility. He placed the ball on the spot and stepped back to the edge of the box.

Roberto gave himself as much of a run-up as his hamstring would allow, but just as he kicked the ball, pain flew up his leg. He lost control of the shot and watched in despair as his penalty sailed over the bar. The Brazil celebrations had already started on the touchline, while Roberto still stood in the box, frozen like a statue.

It was impossible not to feel sympathy for Roberto. He stared at the ground in disbelief, and the 'what-if' nature of his unlucky injury would linger over the final for Italy.

His teammates and coaches tried to find the right words to say to him as he walked off the pitch, but they knew nothing could really ease the heartbreak they were all feeling. The dressing room was silent as the players digested what had just happened. There were tears and hugs and promises to bounce back from this disappointment. The Italians had come so close.

Roberto hadn't quite led the team to the top of the football mountain, but his World Cup brilliance would live on – and so would the sad ending to his 1994 tournament.

CHAPTER 7

ZINEDINE ZIDANE, 1998 WORLD CUP

The hosts in the hotseat

This was the dream. Zinedine Zidane glanced around at the signs and banners promoting the 1998 World Cup. It was all anyone wanted to talk about these days, and he still had to pinch himself to believe that he would be playing *for* France at a World Cup hosted in France.

'The whole country will be cheering you on!' his friends told him.

'No pressure then!' Zinedine replied, laughing. But high expectations were just the reality that summer, and none of the players wanted to let down the millions of fans across the country.

He understood all the excitement. There had been some great teams for *Les Bleus* over the years, but none of them had managed to win the World Cup. Maybe this would be the year where all of that changed.

The French squad was full of talented players, with Fabien Barthez in goal, Marcel Desailly and Lilian Thuram in defence, and Zinedine, Didier Deschamps and Emmanuel Petit running the midfield. If they played as a team, found their best form and got a few lucky bounces, they were capable of going all the way.

But Zinedine let the emotions get to him in France's second group game against Saudi Arabia. Even with a 2–0 lead, he was hungry for more goals, and he knew he had wasted one easy chance in the first half.

He had been dumped on the floor with a few late tackles too, and he lost his cool when another Saudi player slid in around his ankles. Without thinking, Zinedine stamped his studs down and turned to see the referee holding up a red card. Oh no!

All he could do was look at the ground and trudge

slowly off the pitch. It was a lonely walk back to the dressing room, where he sat down and put a towel over his face. How could this be happening?!

France went on to win 4–0, but Zinedine's loss of control got most of the headlines the next day. The red card had raised questions about whether this French team could really rely on him to lead them far in this tournament. When he had thought about leaving his mark on the World Cup, this definitely wasn't what he had in mind.

Zinedine felt terrible. He apologised and accepted the punishment of missing the next match. But his teammates worked hard to cheer him up.

'We need you,' Didier told him. 'You're too important to let this get you down. Put the red card behind you and focus on what comes next. There's still a long way to go in this tournament.'

France survived their Round of 16 match against Paraguay with a late goal, and Zinedine was back for the quarter-final against Italy, where he made amends by scoring in the penalty shoot-out. When Lilian struck two goals in the semi final to beat Croatia,

Zinedine had a World Cup final against Brazil to prepare for.

A line-up in limbo

All week, the France coaches had worked with the defenders on how to stop Ronaldo, Brazil's star striker. They would mark him tightly, and there would always be an extra defender sweeping behind.

Then, just hours before the final's kick-off, Zinedine heard whispers that Ronaldo might not be playing. What?!

The team sheet for Brazil showed Edmundo starting up front instead of Ronaldo. No one seemed to know why, and there were hurried reports back and forth. Was there some kind of health emergency? It had instantly become the top story on all the pre-game TV coverage.

Zinedine didn't let that distract him, though. Really, it didn't matter who would be wearing the Brazil shirt that night, he decided. He knew that if France were going to lift the trophy, he had to be the best player on the pitch.

'This is your night, Zizou,' Didier told him when they finished their warm-up. 'You're at your best in the big games, and the World Cup final is the stage where the stars shine the brightest.'

Zinedine nodded, and Didier could see he had a look in his eye that said, 'I'm ready'.

Even with the nerves swimming around in his stomach, Zinedine had a skill for appearing calm and unflustered. To the outside world, it looked like he was preparing for a weekend league game, not the World Cup final.

But underneath, he was fiercely competitive and he knew what was at stake. It was a chance to put his name in the history books forever, and he liked the sound of that. He had produced some magical performances in his club career so far, but this could cement his place among the top players in the world.

'Enjoy it!' France boss Aimé Jacquet told a nervy dressing room. 'This kind of opportunity doesn't come around often, so give it everything and these fans will carry us the rest of the way.'

When the players stepped into the tunnel, Zinedine

looked up and saw Ronaldo at the back of the Brazil line. So he was playing after all. Game on!

Heading for glory

While the French national anthem boomed around the stadium, Zinedine could feel his heart beating faster. But his first few touches felt good, and he was soon weaving away from defenders.

He was finding lots of space between the Brazil defence and midfield, and that was where he was most dangerous, with clever flicks and testing crosses.

Searching for the first goal, France pushed forward and won a corner. Emmanuel Petit placed the ball next to the corner flag and stepped back to give the signal.

Zinedine waited patiently. He didn't want to make his run too early.

The cross was whipped into the perfect area, and Zinedine was a half-step ahead of his marker. That gave him a running start, and he climbed above another Brazil defender.

Now he just had to make the right contact. He directed a downward header that flew past the keeper faster than even Zinedine expected.

Goooooooooooooooooooooooaaaaaaaaaaaaaaaaaaaaaaallllllllllllllllllllllllllllllllllllll!!!!!!!!!!!!!!!!!!!!!!

The France fans roared. Zinedine looked up into the stands and saw red and blue everywhere.

'Zizooooooooou!' Marcel shouted, jumping on his back.

Zinedine hugged his teammates, then stood up on the advertising boards to get closer to the joyful celebrations in the crowd and accept the applause.

Just before half-time, France won another corner on the opposite side of the pitch. This time, Youri Djorkaeff jogged over.

Like Emmanuel, Youri was great at corners. Zinedine knew the ball would land somewhere in the danger zone. The Brazil players looked like they were ready for the half-time whistle, and they hadn't learned their lesson from the first goal. Again, Zinedine saw that he had room to make a run.

This time, the corner reached him a bit further

out, but that didn't bother him. There was already a lot of pace on the ball, so he just had to direct it on target. He made the perfect contact, thumping his header into the net.

Gooooooooooooooooooooooaaaaaaaaaaaaaaaaaaaaaaallllllllllllllllllllllllllllllllllll!!!!!!!!!!!!!!!!!!!!!!

'You've been keeping all that heading practice a secret!' Youri joked as they high-fived near the corner flag. 'That was a bullet!'

Zinedine grinned. 'Just saving it for the big games, that's all!' he replied.

There were no real signs of a Brazil fightback, and France soaked up the cheers in the second half while the clock ticked down. Emmanuel added a third goal, but the party had already started by then.

Zinedine was the hero. One by one, his teammates rushed over at the final whistle to celebrate with their match-winner.

It had turned into a special night in Paris, and they were all just waiting for the final guest – the World Cup trophy. When it was finally brought out, the crowd got even louder. That made the players turn around to see what all the excitement was about.

'It's here!' Emmanuel called, and they all inched closer to the presentation stage that was being busily assembled.

Seeing the trophy shining on a stand, Zinedine thought about the famous players who had stood where he was now standing. They were joining a long list of great World Cup winners.

If he hadn't already understood what this meant to people across France, he soon realised when the streets were jam-packed for the trophy parade. The crowd was a mix of so many different ages, religions and cultures, all united by their love of football and their pride in this French team's achievement. It was such a beautiful sight that it left Zinedine speechless at first.

'We really did it!' he eventually said, while he and Didier waved to the fans.

CHAPTER 8

RONALDO, 2002 WORLD CUP

A long road back

If he was being honest, Ronaldo had wondered many times whether he would get back to another World Cup at full strength. Since the traumatic 1998 World Cup final, where he really wasn't himself, he had battled through years of injury heartbreak – and his knee had taken some serious punishment.

But two successful operations had given Ronaldo fresh hope, and 'Il Fenomeno' was heading to the 2002 World Cup as the headline act in the Brazil team. Without Ronaldo, their results during the South American qualification phase had fallen short of their best, but he quickly saw there was a lot of potential in the young squad.

'This is going to be fun!' he told Ronaldinho, one of the squad's brightest young stars. The pair had already struck up a fast friendship.

'It sure is, old man!' Ronaldinho replied, grinning.

Ronaldo laughed. He was still only 25, but he felt like one of the senior players when he was surrounded by so many teammates who were early in their careers.

'One of these days, I'll tell you about the 1994 World Cup,' he said. 'That was back in what you'd probably call "my youth"!'

Ronaldo still thought about those days, watching from the bench as a 17-year-old, with Romário and Bebeto running the show. That's when he had really fallen in love with the World Cup.

Now it was his turn to lead the way, and everyone was counting on him. But he would have plenty of help – and defences were about to be introduced to the 3 Rs: not only Ronaldo, but also Rivaldo and Ronaldinho. That trio gave Brazil a chance against anyone.

Ronaldo didn't want to jinx anything, but his body felt good. He still had a burst of pace when he needed it, and he had lost none of his goalscoring instincts. In fact, the coaches gathered round excitedly to watch every Ronaldo shooting drill. The man just never seemed to miss!

After the latest training session, Ronaldo got back to his hotel room, ready for an early night. When he looked in the bathroom mirror, he smiled back at himself.

'We've got a World Cup to win,' he said to himself. 'Bring it on!'

Grins all around

Any hopes that Brazil would immediately transform into a world-beating team were hanging by a thread in the opening game. Trailing 1–0 against Turkey, Ronaldo could sense that the whole tournament might depend on the remaining 45 minutes. If Brazil fell flat here, would a young squad really be able to bounce back?

Time to get us back on track, he thought.

Like any great striker, Ronaldo was always on his toes, trying to get a half-step ahead of his marker. So when Rivaldo shifted the ball onto his left foot, Ronaldo was already sneaking towards the back post. The cross flew past three Turkey defenders, and his gamble paid off. Ronaldo stretched in mid-air and directed the ball into the net.

Gooooooooooooooooooooooooaaaaaaaaaaaaaaaaaaaaaaallllllllllllllllllllllllllllllllllllll!!!!!!!!!!!!!!!!!!!!!

Ronaldo jogged over to celebrate with his teammates, and it was like he had never been away.

The toothy grin.

The wagging finger.

The Brazilian party in the crowd.

That goal settled the nerves, and Rivaldo scored a late penalty to win it.

But Brazil boss Luiz Felipe Scolari, who everyone called Big Phil, wanted to see his team moving the ball faster. 'We're going to play lots of teams with defensive styles,' Big Phil reminded his players. 'When games are like that and space is so tight, we need to be sharper and we need more movement.'

As always with Brazil, there was a promise to play attacking football and carry on the tradition of previous Brazilian teams. Maybe this squad wasn't as talented, but they found an extra gear against China and Costa Rica to cruise to the top of the group.

Against China, Ronaldo anticipated where Cafu would place his cross and tapped the ball into the net.

'Look out, he's baaaaack!' Cafu shouted, laughing.

Against Costa Rica, Ronaldo was in the right place at the right time to bundle a shot past the keeper and put Brazil 1–0 up, before striking again to squeeze in a second goal at the near post. Wonderstrikes from outside the box were great, but he was happy to score the uglier ones, too.

Ronaldo was having the time of his life. He couldn't stop smiling. He was just so thankful to be there playing for his country again at a World Cup. Before the tournament, there had been no way to predict how Ronaldo's knee would handle the intensity of such important games, but this was the best-case scenario. He looked like the best striker in the world again, and fans everywhere were loving it.

The Brazil physios were still monitoring him carefully and arranging extra treatment between games. Ronaldo wasn't going to change a winning formula now.

'Keep doing what you're doing,' he told them, smiling. 'That's got me this far!'

Wins over Belgium and England put Brazil into the semi-final for a rematch with Turkey, and Ronaldo knew what to expect. 'We've got to be patient,' he told his teammates. 'The chances will come.'

Ronaldo even had a special haircut that he hoped would bring Brazil good luck. Most of his head was shaved, except for a patch at the front.

Ronaldinho burst out laughing when he saw it.

'I know you want to show you can still keep up with the cool kids, but this isn't the answer!' he called, giggling.

'Ignore him!' Cafu chimed in. 'As long as you keep scoring, we don't care!'

But the nerves were starting to build at half-time. It was still 0–0, and Turkey were frustrating Brazil again. As always, Ronaldo was prowling for the one chance he needed, and he had a strong feeling that it would take something special to win this semi-final.

Brazil hadn't created that opening yet, so Ronaldo dropped deeper and ended up dribbling into the box from the left wing. He glanced up. Turkey defenders were queuing up for a tackle if he went any further, so he decided to do something they weren't expecting.

Instead of trying to weave past them, he poked an early shot through the crowd. That took everyone by surprise. He didn't hit it hard, but it skidded away from the keeper and into the far corner.

Goooooooooooooooooooooooaaaaaaaaaaaaaaaa aaaaallllllllllllllllllllllllllllllllllll!!!!!!!!!!!!!!!!!!!!!

'You're a genius!' Cafu yelled as he ran to hug Ronaldo.

Big Phil danced on the touchline. The substitutes leapt in the air. Brazil were heading to the 2002 World Cup final.

Banishing the ghosts

So here he was again, preparing for a World Cup final. But Ronaldo felt calmer this time.

All the TV shows were calling it his chance to bury the ghosts of the 1998 final. Ronaldo couldn't deny that, but he tried to keep looking forward. There was no point in reliving that agony. The best medicine would be to beat Germany and give the Brazilian fans a reason for a huge party.

With the adrenaline pumping through his body at kick-off, Ronaldo was ready to run through a wall, if that's what it took. His thigh had been hurting for the last few days, but he had managed to block that out. There was no time to think about that now.

Just as in the semi-final, Ronaldo was tightly marked in the final's first half, and Brazil's attacks were shut down. When Big Phil walked into the dressing room at half-time, it was hard to judge his mood. But then he grinned and looked at his players.

'Come on, I want to see you all smiling too,' he said. 'That's when we're at our best. Let's get back to playing real Brazil football.'

Ronaldo had learned from some amazing coaches in his career, but one of the most basic lessons he ever learned paid off in the second half: gamble on rebounds. First, he fought to win the ball back, shrugging off a German midfielder and laying the ball off to Rivaldo. When Rivaldo fired a low shot from outside the box, Ronaldo followed its path. It was a flash of movement that could distract the goalkeeper – or at least provide some extra pressure.

Oliver Kahn, Germany's star keeper, rarely ever made a mistake, but on this occasion, he fumbled the shot. The rebound bobbled out of his reach, and Ronaldo swooped in to give Brazil the lead.

Goooooooooooooooooooooooaaaaaaaaaaaaaaaaa aaaaallllllllllllllllllllllllllllllllll!!!!!!!!!!!!!!!!!!!!

It certainly wasn't the prettiest goal he had ever scored, but it was one of the most important.

'Let's goooooooo!' he shouted, running towards the fans.

Brazil still wanted a second goal to make the game safe, and Ronaldo joined the attack as the youngster Kléberson broke free on the right wing. He waited as Kléberson cut inside and then made his run just behind Rivaldo.

When Kléberson swept a pass towards Rivaldo,

Ronaldo screamed for his teammate to dummy it. Rivaldo let the ball roll through his legs, and Ronaldo appeared like a blur to smash a first-time shot into the bottom corner.

Goooooooooooooooooooooooaaaaaaaaaaaaaaaaaaaaaallllllllllllllllllllllllllllllllllllllllllll!!!!!!!!!!!!!!!!!!!!!

Ronaldo ran down the touchline towards the Brazil bench with his arms stretched wide. That was his eighth goal at the 2002 World Cup, and his overall total of 12 World Cup goals now matched Pelé's all-time record.

All that was left was the trophy ceremony, where Pelé himself was there to congratulate the Brazil players. Ronaldo grinned as he stepped up to get his medal and then joined his teammates on one side of the stage. Cafu raised the World Cup trophy above his head, and Ronaldo was in the middle of every interview, every hug and every photo.

'To hold the World Cup in my hands is one of the most incredible moments of my life,' he told reporters.

Going home with the Golden Boot award as the tournament's top scorer was a nice bonus, too.

Ronaldo had taken over when Brazil needed him most, but this had been a team effort. When the Brazilians huddled together for a team photo with the World Cup trophy, he was so happy to be sharing the experience with such a special group of teammates.

It had been a long and difficult journey for Ronaldo, but 'Il Fenomeno' was officially back!

CHAPTER 9

FABIO CANNAVARO, 2006 WORLD CUP

Us against the world

The dark clouds swirling above Italy's morning training session symbolised the mood surrounding the team. The 2006 World Cup was just days away, and the players were digesting the news about serious investigations sweeping through Italian football.

As if that wasn't enough, Italy were still trying to shake off the memories of the last World Cup, where they had suffered a shock elimination against South Korea. Consequently, they had limited expectations this time around, but it was Fabio Cannavaro's job to help bring the team together and shut out all the negative noise.

Fabio had taken over as Italian captain from Paolo

Maldini, and he was doing his best to fill those big shoes. When he joined his teammates for the latest meeting with manager Marcello Lippi, he knew they all needed a jolt of energy.

'This is the World Cup, guys,' he said, standing at the front of the room. 'For some of us, this might be our last chance to experience this tournament. We can't get rattled by what people are saying. This is too important.'

He could see his teammates nodding.

'It's us against the world,' he continued. 'If we think like that, we'll be unbreakable.'

Coach Lippi and a few other players spoke up in agreement. There could be no excuses and no regrets.

That conversation seemed to clear the air. The next two practices were the best ones of the week, with more smiles and more focus. Those good vibes carried over to the first game of the tournament, when Italy won 2–0 against Ghana.

Fabio was everywhere across the defence, covering for his teammates and barking instructions to Andrea Pirlo and Simone Perrotta in midfield. The Italians had started slowly at so many World Cups, so it felt good to get the first three points on the board.

Clean sheets and new feats

With Fabio in top form, the Italians had an edge going into the knockout rounds. The defence was giving away so few chances, and the attackers just needed to find one goal to get through.

But that game plan was tested in the second round against Australia when Marco Materazzi was sent off early in the second half. Fabio felt bad for Marco, but his job now was to hold the Italy defence together. These were the situations he loved, with Australia pushing forward and Italy throwing themselves into tackles and blocks to keep them out.

Australia tried everything to break through, but Fabio was there again and again with a last-ditch tackle or a crucial clearance. When Italy won a late penalty on a rare attack, Francesco Totti made no mistake, clinching the kind of 1–0 win that Fabio dreamed about.

'That's what we do!' he shouted, hugging keeper

Gianluigi Buffon. 'What an effort!'

It was Italy's third clean sheet of the tournament, and there was soon a fourth – their 3–0 quarter-final win against Ukraine. Injuries and suspensions were forcing Coach Lippi to reshuffle his defence, but Fabio was the rock. As long as he was there, the Italians felt safe.

So often, it was the star attackers who got the biggest spotlight at the World Cup, but Fabio was putting his name in those conversations, too.

The game of his life

It was going to take something special to beat Germany, the tournament hosts, in the semi-final. Fabio had watched enough of their matches to know that they had quality players all over the pitch.

Sure enough, Italy were under pressure from the opening minutes, and Fabio was soon screaming to organise the defence. He slid to block one shot, then won an important header. He wiped the sweat from his forehead and then Germany attacked again.

All of this early action meant that Fabio was into

the rhythm of the match quickly – and into that elite state where he was playing the game one second faster than everyone else. He anticipated passes, moved into position to win headers and covered behind his teammates. There was no way through for the Germans.

'Fantastic!' Coach Lippi told him at half-time, shaking his captain's hand. 'It's like there are three Fabios out there.'

Fabio could see the Germans hesitate when they saw him standing in their way. Sometimes they tripped over the ball. Other times they decided to go backwards instead of getting too close to him.

But all the heroic defending would be wasted if Italy failed to create chances at the other end of the pitch. With a penalty shoot-out just minutes away, Fabio watched while Andrea controlled a clearance at the edge of the Germany box.

'Shoot!' Fabio shouted.

But there were lots of white shirts rushing towards Andrea. Instead, he threaded a pass to Fabio Grosso, who whipped a curling shot into the far corner.

Yes! Yes! Yes!

Fabio jumped in the air. It had taken 119 minutes, but Italy finally had their reward. The German fans were silent and Fabio reminded his teammates that the game wasn't over yet.

'We've worked too hard to blow it now,' he said. 'Stay switched on, and don't take any risks.'

Germany thumped a desperate cross into the box, but Fabio was ready for it. He got there first to win the header, then followed the looping ball into midfield. Even though a German player was waiting to control it, only one person was going to win that challenge.

Fabio powered forward, won possession and set up a breakaway goal for Alessandro Del Piero.

Game over!

Fabio was exhausted. With his hands on his knees, he accepted the congratulations from his teammates and the German squad. He had been the best player on the pitch, and he couldn't remember playing a better game than this one.

A dream come true

Fabio didn't take any of it for granted. It was such an honour to lead the team out as captain for a World Cup final, and it made him emotional just thinking about it. He was so proud of what Italy had achieved over the last few weeks, and now they had to finish the job in the final. It wouldn't be easy against France, though.

'One more hurdle to go,' he told his teammates, while they huddled together before kick-off. 'Give it everything you've got.'

Italy hadn't yet conceded a goal by an opponent in the whole tournament – just one own goal in the group stage – so it was a shock when France took the lead after Marco gave away a penalty.

Fortunately, Marco made up for it with an equaliser, and everyone could breathe again. Fabio signalled to his teammates to settle down. They had only played 18 minutes so far.

After half-time, Italy were hanging on. Fabio was pointing and reorganising, but the French attacks kept coming, and he needed all of his experience to stay tight to Thierry Henry. It was a similar story in extra time, with Fabio defending deep and letting the minutes tick by.

Zidane was sent off for headbutting Marco, but there wasn't time for Italy to take advantage. The referee blew his whistle and Fabio took a deep breath. The 2006 World Cup would be decided on penalties.

Fabio knew he wouldn't be one of the first five penalty takers for Italy, but he was as nervous as anyone. He high-fived Gianluigi, then joined his teammates. Linking arms, they all stood on the halfway line. No one spoke.

Penalty after penalty flew into the net, until a French kick cannoned off the crossbar. Suddenly, that man Grosso stepped up for another crucial moment. This could be it. The Italians were ready to explode.

When the ball flew into the net, Fabio was in the middle of the blue shirts racing to celebrate with Grosso and Gianluigi. It was pure joy as he bounced from hug to hug.

After all the off-field drama, which was continuing to develop back home, the Italian squad had delivered their own response with one of the grittiest ever World

Cup runs. They had done what had seemed impossible a month earlier.

It was just the beginning of the major awards for Fabio. His World Cup masterclasses were recognised with the FIFA World Player of the Year and Ballon d'Or awards for 2006. Those were rare achievements for a defender – and further confirmation that Fabio had put himself alongside the greatest defenders to ever play the game.

CHAPTER 10

ANDRÉS INIESTA, 2010 WORLD CUP

A race against time

The countdown was on! The 2010 World Cup was just weeks away, and the best players on the planet would soon be travelling to South Africa for the tournament. Andrés Iniesta was watching the calendar as closely as anyone. The Barcelona midfield maestro was still recovering from a serious thigh injury that had wrecked his club season, but in the gym, he was focusing on the World Cup.

'I've got to be ready!' he would repeat to himself as he turned up the music and went through another set of exercises.

Andrés had done a lot of winning lately. He was

part of the Spain squad that had won Euro 2008, and he had been one of Barca's stars in an amazing 2008–09 season where they clinched the Spanish league, cup and Champions League for a stunning Treble.

But the World Cup was different. There was something magnetic about that tournament and its famous golden trophy. Spain had never won it, despite having some good teams, and Andrés might never get a better chance to change that fact.

Vicente del Bosque, the Spain manager, checked in regularly for updates while Andrés got closer and closer to full fitness. Vicente would soon have to name his final squad for the tournament, and there was no one who could replace what Andrés brought to the team. Even a half-fit Andrés could be a dangerous weapon, and Spanish fans everywhere were crossing their fingers that their little magician would be on the plane.

'We'll leave the decision as late as possible,' Vicente told him. 'Everyone knows we're not the same team without you!'

The clock kept ticking as Andrés progressed from jogging to running to short sprints.

When he passed the last fitness test, he grinned and high-fived the physios. What a relief!

'South Africa, here I come!' he shouted, picking up the phone to call Vicente.

Shaking off the rust

Even after playing in so many big games, Andrés was still nervous ahead of the first World Cup group game. It was never easy to come back from an injury. He had to learn to trust his leg again and catch up with the speed of the game – and he was trying to do all of that with the expectations of a World Cup hanging over him.

'Just focus on one pass at a time,' Xavi said, with a wink. 'Don't look too far ahead.'

Andrés nodded. It felt good to have his Barcelona teammates around him. Xavi, Carles Puyol, Gerard Piqué, Sergio Busquets, Pedro and David Villa were all in the squad, so at least that part felt normal. Together, they had already overcome so many obstacles.

After winning Euro 2008, Spain were among the favourites again, but there were still some ups and downs in the group stage, especially for Andrés. He wanted to skip through the hotel when he was named in the starting line-up for the opening game against Switzerland, but his heart sank on the pitch when he felt a pain in his thigh.

'No! No! No!' he yelled, slapping the turf. He thought about the long hours of treatment over the last few months. Was all his hard work for nothing?

But it was a false alarm. 'Nothing is torn or broken,' the physios explained. 'You just need to rest it.'

Andrés didn't like the sound of 'rest', but overall, this was a huge relief. His tournament wasn't over. Maybe he could even play in Spain's next game. But when he limped across his hotel room the next morning, he knew that was too ambitious.

The instructions were clear: *Give your body some time to heal.*

'You'll be thanking me when you're playing in the World Cup final!' the Spain physio said when he saw the sad look on Andrés' face at their treatment session.

Those words stuck with Andrés. He was back for the last group game against Chile, scoring the key goal in a 2–1 victory and gliding around the pitch like a man determined to keep the World Cup adventure alive.

'If you're on the pitch, we can beat anyone!' Vicente said, shaking Andrés' hand on the touchline.

Knockout round wins over Portugal, Paraguay and Germany sent Spain all the way to the World Cup final, and now only the Netherlands stood between Andrés and his team and the biggest prize in football.

High kicks and low blows

'Ouch!' Xavi yelled, tumbling to the ground. A flying Dutch boot had just whacked him in the chest, and the tension in the stadium flew up another level.

Andrés rushed over to check on his friend, and other Spanish players ran to the referee. The World Cup final was getting out of control.

'How many times?!' Andrés muttered, shaking his head.

This was just the latest Netherlands foul. Andrés

had dealt with his share of the physicality, too. A pull on his shirt. A shove in the back. A late tackle after he had already passed the ball. There was a whistle every few seconds.

This wasn't the type of game that Spain liked to play. In fact, it felt more like one of the heated Barcelona vs Real Madrid matches. But Andrés had played in enough bruising games to know how to handle it. Opponents had tried this kind of approach before, and usually it backfired.

'Keep your cool!' he shouted to his teammates, reminding them not to be provoked by the late Dutch tackles. 'Just stick together and play our way.'

The worst possible reaction would be to lash out and receive a red card. That would give the Netherlands exactly what they wanted. Spain had to show they had the mental strength to get through this test – and if they did that, Andrés knew their football talent would shine through.

Vicente was signalling for calm, too. He appeared on the touchline and waved Andrés over.

'Stay a little deeper to help us move the ball away

from the pressure,' he told Andrés. 'Then when they start to get tired, that's when we'll pounce.'

The dream moment

As the game ticked towards the end of extra time, it was still 0–0. Andrés glanced up at the scoreboard in the stadium. It was now or never. He was tired, but this was the World Cup final. He could sleep later.

There was still time for one more attack, and Andrés forced his legs to make another run into the box. Fernando Torres's cross from the left wing didn't quite reach him, but at least Cesc Fàbregas got to the loose ball.

'Cesc! Cesc!' Andrés screamed, as loudly as he could. Somehow, he had a yard of space.

Cesc heard him, and Andrés knew this was his moment. He took a quick touch to cushion Cesc's pass, and the ball bounced up perfectly for a half-volley.

Then the rest happened in slow motion. Out of the corner of his eye, he could see a Dutch defender charging towards him. But he was going to be too late.

Andrés looked up at the net, picked his spot and fired a shot across the keeper with all the power he had left in his body.

When the ball hit the back of the net, Andrés froze for a second, and then the emotions hit him all at once.

Gooooooooooooooooooooooaaaaaaaaaaaaaaaaaaaaaallllllllllllllllllllllllllllllllllllllllll!!!!!!!!!!!!!!!!!!!!!

'Surely now, Spain have won the World Cup for the first time!' the commentator roared.

Having looked over his shoulder to check that there wasn't an offside flag, Andrés set off sprinting towards the corner flag. Suddenly, he wasn't tired anymore.

Then he remembered. The vest. He took off his shirt so the cameras could see the message he had written on his vest before the game. It was a message for Dani Jarque, his fellow player and friend who had died the previous year, 2009. This goal was for him.

By now, the Spain substitutes and coaches were running up the touchline with their arms in the air, and his teammates got to him even sooner, burying him at the bottom of a big pile.

'Andrés, your right foot just won us the World Cup!' Carles Puyol shouted, wrapping him in a big hug.

At the final whistle, Andrés dropped to his knees, thinking about what Spain had just achieved and how close he had been to missing out on this whole adventure. The red section of the crowd had already started the party, and soon the players were joining in. He spotted his girlfriend, Anna, and saw the tears of joy rolling down her cheeks. Andrés waved and blew her a kiss. Anna had been by his side throughout his long recovery from injury, and he wouldn't have been there without her.

Andrés got one of the loudest cheers when he stepped forward for his medal. When his country needed him most, he had delivered. Holding the World Cup trophy and walking around the pitch with his teammates, he knew this was a night he would never forget.

CHAPTER 11

TIM HOWARD, 2014 WORLD CUP

Underdogs

For Tim Howard, the road to the 2014 World Cup in Brazil had been long and winding. The American goalkeeper had started his career in the US league before transfers to Manchester United and Everton in the Premier League. Year after year, he had worked hard to become a top-tier goalie.

Now Tim was playing in the second round of the world's biggest tournament against a dangerous Belgium team. He had more than 100 caps for his country, but this was still a daunting challenge. Luckily, he lived for these situations.

'If the USA are going to pull off an upset here, it

starts with Tim Howard,' one of the commentators said during the pre-game build-up.

Tim didn't need anyone to remind him about that. The USA were fighting to prove they could go toe-to-toe with the world's top teams, and this showdown against the Belgians was a perfect opportunity to make a statement.

At least Tim was in good form. His saves had helped the Americans beat Ghana and draw with Portugal during the group stage, and he was an important veteran presence in the dressing room. They would be relying on him more than ever in this game.

As usual, he had watched countless video clips with the coaches. He wanted to take mental notes on where the Belgian players liked to place their shots and what to expect from corners and free kicks. That way, he could bark out instructions during the game.

'We may have to deal with some long spells of defending today,' he told his teammates as they reviewed some last-minute instructions. 'But we'll be fine as long as we communicate with each other.

We've got to stay with their strikers and watch for midfielders joining the attack.'

'And if Belgium get through, Tim will be there to stop them,' interrupted Clint Dempsey, the USA captain. 'That should make all of us feel more confident.'

Just then, an official knocked loudly on the dressing room door. It was time for the walk down to the tunnel. Tim picked up his gloves and water bottle, then fist-bumped his teammates. The waiting was over. Shouts of 'Let's go!' echoed down the corridor.

Saving the day – again, and again

Tim could tell from the first ten minutes of the game that it was going to be a long night for him. Led by Eden Hazard and Kevin De Bruyne, Belgium were surging through the USA defence and creating scoring chances.

He saved two shots with his legs to rescue his defenders, then tipped another over the bar acrobatically.

'We're giving them too much space!' he yelled,

trying to rally his teammates. They were backing off so far that Belgium could shoot whenever they wanted.

But sometimes it was better to be busy. Rather than standing around and battling to stay alert, Tim was in the action constantly. His reflexes were sharp, and he was careful not to give the Belgian strikers any rebounds from long-range shots.

He could see the frustration growing for Belgium, too. They couldn't believe they hadn't scored yet. At the same time, the noise from the American fans was getting louder. They were cheering every save and waving flags behind the net.

The second half followed the same script. The USA were trapped in their own half, and Tim made two brilliant one-on-one saves to keep the game goalless. How long could he keep up this solo act?!

'Now you're just showing off!' Hazard joked when Tim just barely got a stud on the ball to deflect it wide.

With every save, Tim felt more unbeatable. The ball seemed bigger and the net seemed smaller. When he took a few strides forward to narrow the angle, there wasn't much space for the attackers to aim at.

His defenders were starting to tire, but Tim was there to deal with the danger. He stretched to push away a curler from Hazard, then blocked two more low shots from the Belgium strikers.

But the USA were constantly trying to catch their breath. Tim took as long as he could on each goal kick to give his teammates a chance to get back in position or stretch cramping muscles. Even with substitutes providing fresher legs, Belgium seemed to be first to every loose ball.

At last, during extra time, the clean sheet was ripped away from Tim. Kevin De Bruyne and Romelu Lukaku finally found a way past him, and the American fans were silenced. Tim had done everything he could.

But there was still time left on the clock, and Tim hadn't given up hope. He stood on the edge of his box and watched as the USA pulled one goal back and set up a dramatic finish. They were inches away from an equaliser in the final seconds, but there would be no fairytale comeback.

It took a long time for Tim to drag himself off the pitch. He didn't want to believe that the USA's World Cup was over. The Belgium players were quick to praise his incredible saves, and his own teammates wrapped him in hugs.

'I thought that was Superman in goal tonight!' Hazard said to Tim, shaking his hand. 'That was an unbelievable performance!'

'You kept us in it, man,' Clint added while they walked towards the tunnel together. 'I just wish we could have found another goal at the end to pay you back.'

Record-setter

Tim couldn't hide his sadness as he took off his gloves and slumped down in the dressing room. For a few minutes, no one spoke.

'We were so close,' he said, finally and quietly.

His teammates nodded in agreement. Sure, Belgium had dominated the match, but the USA could have snatched it away from them with a few luckier bounces.

'We dreamed and we fell short of our dream,' Tim told reporters. 'It's heartbreaking.'

He wasn't sure what else to say. All the emotions were still too raw.

It was only when Tim was on the team bus that he found out about the new record he had set. One of the coaches stopped next to him in the aisle with a sheet of paper in his hands.

'Just thought you might like to see this,' he said, passing it to Tim. 'I know it doesn't make things better, but it's pretty remarkable.'

Tim looked at the sheet, and his eyebrows shot up in surprise. Among the notes about the game, it showed that he had set a new tournament record: *sixteen saves in a single World Cup game.*

Was it really that many? Tim went back through some of those key stops in his head. He stopped counting after he reached 12. He trusted the people who kept track of these things.

#ThingsTimHowardCanSave even became a trending topic as the world reacted to Tim's masterclass.

Of course, Tim didn't want to think about anything like that when the loss was still so fresh. After all, he was just doing his job, and he would have happily swapped all of those saves for a USA win.

But, like all records, it was cool to have a place in the history books. Despite that final result, Tim knew that he had stepped up with the game of his life when it mattered most.

Growing the game

As the weeks passed, something else became very clear – the team's success in Brazil had been about more than just winning games and qualifying for the knockout rounds. More and more people believed that the 2014 World Cup also marked a big step in the popularity of 'soccer' across the USA.

The nation had fallen in love with this fearless team and their gritty personalities. With millions of Americans tuning in to watch the matches on TV, including more than 16 million for the USA-Belgium match, it was a huge boost for the growth of the game. Maybe that would be the spark to take Major

League Soccer – or MLS for short – to the next level.

When the pain of the USA's exit had eased a little, Tim could look back proudly on what the team had achieved. They had set a new standard and inspired young players across the country on their own football journeys.

'There's something really cool to build on now,' he told his friends. 'We've just got to keep the momentum going. One day, the USA really could be lifting that trophy.'

CHAPTER 12

CRISTIANO RONALDO, 2018 WORLD CUP

A man on a mission

After Portugal's run to glory at Euro 2016, Cristiano Ronaldo knew that anything was possible, especially when he was playing at his best. His trophy cabinet was stacked with individual and team awards, but was that enough to make him the GOAT?

That was a debate with no clear answer, despite endless discussions around the football world. Cristiano and Lionel Messi were locked in a battle as two of the leading candidates, and lifting the World Cup trophy might finally be a way to separate them.

So, Portugal arrived at the 2018 World Cup in Russia with some extra attention. Cristiano welcomed that. He spent most of his life in the spotlight these days, and he had worked hard to push Portugal into the select group of tournament contenders.

Now he had to deliver, and he had a talented group of players around him on this mission. Pepe, João Moutinho and Ricardo Quaresma were all experienced, established stars, and they had all tasted major tournament glory together two years ago.

Cristiano went through his usual intense workouts and encouraged his teammates to take every practice as seriously as he did. That disciplined attitude had worked well for him over the years, keeping him at the top of the game while other players had begun to fade.

'Come on, guys, be sharper!' he called during a training drill that had become sloppy. 'We're better than this!'

His teammates immediately refocused. No one wanted to let Cristiano down.

By the time that the Portugal squad finished their latest training session, they were in a confident mood, and Cristiano felt good about their chances of a deep World Cup run.

Facing good friends

Cristiano grinned when he thought about Portugal's first group game. They would be facing Spain – and some of his own Real Madrid teammates, like Sergio Ramos, Dani Carvajal, Marco Asensio and Isco. Texts were soon pinging back and forth between them.

'I can't go easy on you just because we're friends,' Cristiano joked.

'Just be ready for Sergio's flying tackles!' Isco shot back.

But it was all serious business when they stepped into the tunnel. Cristiano was in the zone, and he stared straight ahead, trying to clear his mind for the battle ahead. Some of the Spain players were his friends, but today he had to think of them as the opposition.

Cristiano had a good feeling about this game, and he was soon causing panic in the Spain defence. When he got the ball on the left wing in the opening minutes, he didn't hesitate.

Nacho Fernández, the Real Madrid defender, was in front of him, and he liked that matchup. Cristiano saw Nacho was already backpedalling, and that was just an invitation to dribble into the box. He sped forward, froze Nacho with a stepover and then felt a clip on his ankle as he skipped through. Penalty!

Cristiano bounced back up and put the ball on the spot. He calmly fired the ball into the net to give Portugal the lead.

Goooooooooooooooooooooooaaaaaaaaaaaaaaaaa aaaaallllllllllllllllllllllllllllllllllllllll!!!!!!!!!!!!!!!!!!!!!

He ran towards the corner flag, and stroked his chin. Commentators and fans around the world were quick to suggest it was a reminder that Cristiano was in the GOAT conversation.

He followed it with his famous *SIIIIIIIIIIUUUUUUUUU* celebration, jumping and spinning in mid-air.

'Sorry, man, I had to do it!' Cristiano told Nacho as he ran back to the halfway line.

Worth a shot?

When Spain hit back, Cristiano brushed it off. There was a lot of time left in the game, and he knew there would be more opportunities. As Portugal captain, he demanded a lot from the rest of the squad, but he also understood that he had to set the example when the game was tight. This was one of those times.

Later in the first half, he got the ball on the edge of the box and glanced up to see where his teammates were. There was no one in space, so he decided it was worth a shot. Cristiano was never shy about testing the keeper with long-range efforts. He had missed plenty in his career – but if you don't shoot, you don't score.

He instantly knew he had scuffed this one, though. Instead of fizzing and swerving like his usual rockets, the ball skimmed along the ground, straight towards the keeper. It was as slow as a back pass.

Cristiano was about to slap his thigh in disappointment – but hang on. He watched in shock as Spain keeper David de Gea misjudged it. The ball hit his knee and trickled into the net.

Goooooooooooooooooooooooooaaaaaaaaaaaaaaaaaaaaaaallllllllllllllllllllllllllllllllll!!!!!!!!!!!!!!!!!!!!!

Well, they all count, Cristiano thought. He still

celebrated it as if it was a wonderstrike, and his teammates were soon wrapping him in hugs and laughing at his good luck.

'Teams are in trouble if you're even scoring with your worst shots!' Pepe teased, putting his arm round Cristiano. 'I never score when I shoot like that!'

'That's what I meant to do,' Cristiano replied, with a wink. 'It was all the really slow backspin I put on the shot to fool the keeper.'

He was joking, of course, but the goal was a big boost. Any tournament winner needed a little luck, and that error by Spain had given Portugal hope. It was Cristiano's fifth career World Cup goal – and he wasn't done yet.

Bringing home the match ball

There were more twists and turns ahead as Spain fought back to take a 3–2 lead, and Portugal looked to Cristiano for one more moment of magic. This was why he worked so hard in the gym – so that he still had the energy to take advantage whenever opponents were tiring.

With two minutes left, Portugal got a free kick in shooting range, and there was no question about who would take it. None of his teammates even thought about asking. Cristiano lined up the ball and stepped back dramatically. As usual, he took one deep breath, breathed out and waited for the referee's whistle.

Then Cristiano jogged forward and struck the ball, just like so many times on the training ground. He got the perfect whip and dip, curling it over the wall. 'That's got a chance,' he thought, as soon as it left his boot.

The keeper was helpless as the ball dropped just under the crossbar.

Goooooooooooooooooooooooooaaaaaaaaaaaaaaaaaa aaaaalllllllllllllllllllllllllllllllllllll!!!!!!!!!!!!!!!!!!!!

Yes! Cristiano raced off to celebrate. What a goal! What a game!

'Cristiano to the rescue again!' Pepe shouted. 'How do you do it?!'

After handshakes with Sergio and the rest of the Spain players, Cristiano high-fived his teammates.

He was so impressed with the resilience they had all shown.

On his way towards the tunnel, he called to the referee and pointed to the match ball. He wanted that for his collection.

'I've got to have a souvenir from a World Cup hat-trick!' he said with a grin.

Before he could go through his recovery process, Cristiano had his typical post-game commitments. He stepped in front of the cameras, and microphones and recording devices appeared out of thin air.

'I'm very happy,' he explained. 'That was a personal best. Now we have to think about the next match. It's going to be hard, but our goal is to win and to move on from the group stage.'

Spain's coach was equally impressed. 'When you are playing a player like Ronaldo, these things can happen,' he said.

Back in the dressing room, Cristiano found out about even more records that he had set. Thirty-three years old, he had just become the oldest player ever to score a hat-trick at a World Cup, and only the fourth player in history to score in four separate World Cups.

'Not bad!' he said, smiling.

It was a promising start, but Portugal's summer would end in disappointment – with a second-round loss to Uruguay. Cristiano was crushed. He replayed key parts of the game in his head, and he still couldn't believe the result. Portugal had taken 20 shots that day and scored just one goal.

But if there was one silver lining for Cristiano in the 2018 World Cup, it was the unforgettable memory of his hat-trick. It was one of the most inspirational performances of his career, and a reminder that he could still take over in the biggest games.

CHAPTER 13

HARRY KANE, 2018 WORLD CUP

A new-look England?

No one needed to remind Harry Kane about England's history of failures at major tournaments. He had heard all the stories, and he knew all the details, from David Beckham to David Seaman to Wayne Rooney.

As a fan, he had watched England's disappointing World Cup exits in 2002, 2006 and 2010, and he had only just made his first Premier League start for Tottenham when England crumbled at the 2014 World Cup. Those were huge letdowns when the squad looked more than capable of competing with the best teams on the planet.

But now Harry had the chance to lead a new, happier chapter for his country. This was a fresh start, led by manager Gareth Southgate, and Harry had played a big part in the emergence of a different mood around the England camp. As captain, he set the example for others to follow, and his goalscoring record put him among the best strikers in the world.

As the 2018 World Cup approached, he couldn't wait to build on that reputation still further. For once, England didn't have the extra pressure of being called 'contenders'. After all the tournament heartbreak of past years, there seemed to be an acceptance that other countries were playing at a higher level, and Harry was comfortable with the team flying under the radar. England could probably never be called underdogs, but they were in a position to surprise people.

'Go out there and play with freedom,' Gareth explained to the squad at their hotel in Russia. 'Wearing the England shirt is one of the greatest honours you can have in your careers, and we've got a whole country desperate to get behind a team that's fearless and connected. Let's make them proud.'

Harry liked the sound of that. He was coming off a Premier League season where he had scored 30 goals for Tottenham, and now he was desperate to fire England towards the World Cup final. He wouldn't be doing it alone, but he understood that the team was relying on him to make life miserable for opposition defenders.

'We can talk about a new era for England, but we've got to prove it with good performances on the pitch,' he told his parents when they called one evening. 'The build-up has been great here, and we just want to get the games started now!'

But there were no easy wins at the World Cup – and that was clear during the opening group game against Tunisia.

A last-gasp rescue

Harry had imagined what it would be like to lead out the team at the World Cup, but nothing could have prepared him for the pride and excitement he felt as he walked down the tunnel. It was surreal. He heard the clatter of studs behind him, and a wave of noise hit him when the fans reacted to their heroes stepping onto the pitch.

'Here we go!' he thought.

Instead of just passing a ball around for a couple of minutes like the rest of his teammates, Harry jogged forward for the coin toss, shaking hands with the referee, assistant referees and the Tunisia captain.

Harry loved the extra responsibility and he really wanted to be a good leader, but scoring goals was his biggest strength. He had a gift for being in the right place at the right time, and he gave England a dream start by pouncing on the rebound when John Stones's header was saved.

Gooooooooooooooooooooooaaaaaaaaaaaaaaaaa aaaaallllllllllllllllllllllllllllllllllll!!!!!!!!!!!!!!!!!!!!

It seemed like England had everything under control. But they couldn't find a second goal, and Tunisia punished them with a shock equaliser.

'Keep your heads up, lads!' Harry called. 'Let's go and get another goal.'

But the minutes ticked by, and he could sense the nervous energy in the crowd. Was this the same old England story at major tournaments? That's what the fans were probably thinking.

Harry had to push those thoughts away. He had to keep trying. In the second minute of added time, England won a corner. This would be one of their last chances, and Harry just hoped that Kieran Trippier would put the cross in a dangerous area.

Kieran didn't let him down. A flick-on at the near post sent the ball across the box, and yet again Harry's instincts kicked in. He had drifted into space at the back post and nodded in a simple header.

Gooooooooooooooooooooooaaaaaaaaaaaaaaaaaaaaaallllllllllllllllllllllllllllllllllllllll!!!!!!!!!!!!!!!!!!!!!

Yes!!! He raced off to celebrate feeling a mix of joy and relief. It had to be the winning goal. All of his teammates followed him and piled on top. Once again, Harry had saved the day for England!

'Harry is a top, top striker,' Gareth told the reporters. 'Good teams score late goals.'

Back in the dressing room, there were hugs and

smiles. It was a winning start, but Harry knew that the scoreline should never have been so close.

'That was a wake-up call for us,' Harry told his teammates. 'We've got to take our chances in the next game.'

Chasing the Golden Boot

After the two goals against Tunisia, Harry was an even more popular pick to be the tournament's top scorer. But he wasn't going to ease up as England prepared to face Panama.

'Strikers have to be a bit greedy sometimes,' Harry said. 'I'm not satisfied just because I've scored a couple of goals. I want more.'

He got his wish against the Panama defence: England fired in goal after goal.

A penalty into the top corner. Bang!

Another penalty into the top corner. Bang!

A deflection off his heel that looped into the net. Thanks!

Harry's hat trick helped England to a 6–1 victory. He could sense the excitement from the England fans at the tournament, as well as all the texts and videos he got from his friends and family watching at home. The whole country was buzzing while the team prepared for the knockout rounds.

Harry would also make a big difference in England's second-round game against Colombia. When he was pulled down in the box at a corner, the referee awarded a penalty. With a confident run-up, Harry tucked it past the Colombia goalkeeper.

Goooooooooooooooooooooooaaaaaaaaaaaaaaaa aaaaallllllllllllllllllllllllllllllll!!!!!!!!!!!!!!!!!!!!!

England weren't safe yet, though – Colombia scored a late goal, and England would have to win a penalty shoot-out to keep their World Cup hopes alive. Shoot-outs hadn't been kind to England in the past, but this was another chance to show that times had changed.

Gareth had insisted that the players practice penalties regularly to be ready for this kind of test, and Harry was ruthless with his kick to get England off to a good start. Jordan Pickford made a great save, and England managed to hold their nerve. They had reached the quarter-final.

'It shows what we're made of,' Harry told reporters. 'Penalties have been terrible for us over the years – of course we know that – and to step up when it mattered and do what we did, I'm so proud of everyone involved. We're a young squad, but we learnt a lot out there today.'

After a 2–0 win in the quarter-final against Sweden, Harry could see how far the team had come. Instead of going into these big games with doubts, England were getting the upper hand and expecting to win. It also helped when big Harry Maguire was coming up for corners and scoring headers.

England were within touching distance of the World Cup final, but they fell just short against Croatia, whose extra-time goal felt like a punch in the stomach. When the referee blew the final whistle, Harry crouched and looked down at the pitch. England's amazing adventure was over, but the fans stayed behind to cheer loudly. They had loved every minute of the team's brave performances.

'It's been an amazing run, but it hurts to lose,' Harry admitted after the game, with the pain of the loss starting to sink in. 'We wanted to go on and win it, and we thought we had enough to go through. But it wasn't to be.'

Back in the dressing room, Gareth tried to console his players. Like Harry, he was so proud of what the team had achieved. 'We'll be back,' he told them. 'This is just the beginning for us.'

Harry's goalscoring heroics, particularly in the group stage, won him the Golden Boot, with six goals in the tournament. That award couldn't make up for missing out on the final, but it would be a permanent reminder of what England had achieved at the 2018 World Cup.

CHAPTER 14

LIONEL MESSI, 2022 WORLD CUP

A golden opportunity

Argentina's Lionel 'Leo' Messi had achieved so much in his career. His list of trophies included the Champions League, La Liga and the Copa America, plus a massive collection of individual awards. But when it came to the World Cup, victory had always slipped through his hands.

Leo had come close in 2014, only losing to Germany in the final. He knew by 2022 that time was running out. He would keep trying, provided he felt fit enough. Even so, he had to accept the possibility that the 2022 World Cup might be his last chance to lift the trophy.

Argentina arrived in Qatar with a strong squad, and Leo could see that it wouldn't all rest on his shoulders. But a shock 2–1 loss to Saudi Arabia in the first group game brought out all the Messi doubters, despite Leo scoring Argentina's goal from the penalty spot.

'This one hurts, but we can't lose confidence in each other,' Leo told his teammates in a stunned dressing room. 'It's one loss. We're not going to give up.'

Argentina couldn't afford another setback, and boss Lionel Scaloni didn't need to remind Leo that they were counting on him. Fortunately, Leo scored the first goal in a 2–0 win over Mexico, and then they swept past Poland to top the group. Phew!

'What was everyone so worried about?' Leo joked.

'Yeah, we weren't sweating at all after that first game,' Ángel Di María added sarcastically.

The players could smile about it now, but it had been a draining week. A group stage elimination would have been a complete disaster.

With Leo leading the way, Argentina had some momentum now. His unstoppable curler helped to eliminate Australia in the second round, then he netted his penalty in the shoot-out win over the Netherlands.

But he put on his biggest masterclass so far in the semi-final against Croatia, turning defenders inside out with some vintage dribbling and sending Argentina through to the final. For Leo, it would be a second chance to achieve his World Cup dream.

The perfect start

Argentina had come a long way since their wobbly start to the tournament, but it would all count for nothing if they didn't show up in the final.

All eyes were on Leo from the minute he arrived at the stadium. The cameras zoomed in during the warm-up, and once again when he stood at the front of the Argentina line in the tunnel. But he was used to all that. His mind was clear, and he was ready.

When he thought back to the 2014 final, he regretted not finding more ways to get involved. He wasn't going to let the same thing happen in the 2022 final. This time, Argentina made a flying start against France. They pushed forward to take charge of the opening minutes and kept the pressure on. Then Ángel was pulled down in the box, and the referee pointed to the spot.

That gave Leo his first chance to make an impact on this final. He had missed some big penalties in the past, but he always believed in himself. After a few patient steps, he drilled the ball into the bottom corner.

Goooooooooooooooooooooooaaaaaaaaaaaaaaaaa aaaaallllllllllllllllllllllllllllllllllll!!!!!!!!!!!!!!!!!!!!!

But Argentina didn't sit back and protect the lead. They went for the knockout blow instead, launching a lightning counterattack. Leo played his part in the move, and Ángel steered a first-time shot past the keeper. 2–0.

An experienced French team looked rattled. They were losing every 50-50 ball, and their shoulders were slumping. Leo encouraged his teammates to keep snapping into tackles, and the Argentina fans sang even louder while the clock ticked down.

With just over ten minutes to go, there was no sign

of a comeback from France. Argentina were in full control – until suddenly, they weren't.

A two-minute collapse

Watching from the halfway line, Leo couldn't believe what he was seeing. From being on the brink of lifting the World Cup trophy, Argentina faltered at the worst possible moment. Maybe they let their concentration slip. Maybe it was the nerves. Either way, it was a meltdown.

France scored two goals in just two minutes to turn the game upside down, and Argentina's dream final was slowly shifting towards a nightmare. Leo was in shock, but he had to help Argentina regroup. The match wasn't over yet.

It was almost a relief when he heard the final whistle and had a chance to process what had just happened. Leo stood with Ángel and Julián Alvarez on the pitch before extra-time began, and he guzzled water in preparation for another 30 minutes.

'Football can be cruel, man,' Leo said, shaking his head.

'I just didn't see that coming at all,' Ángel added. He had been subbed off before the collapse, and now he could only watch from the touchline.

Argentina had been so close, and it was impossible not to think about that. They could have been celebrating with the fans by now. But Coach Scaloni did his best to make them concentrate on their next attack and their next chance. Leo stretched his calves and his hamstrings to try to keep the cramp away.

'Now we've got to do it all again,' Leo told his teammates. 'Let's go and win it!'

On top of the world

With extra time, there was always the dilemma of whether chasing a goal was worth the risk of conceding one yourselves. But Leo understood that Argentina had to take that chance. They had to find a way to respond after France's comeback.

Leo was mostly walking around when France had the ball, and that meant he could save up his energy for Argentina attacks. When striker Lautaro Martínez got behind the defence, he thumped a shot from a tight angle and the rebound bounced loose in the box. Leo was there in a flash, and he poked it towards the net. A desperate French clearance was a second too late, and the referee signalled that the ball had crossed the line.

Goooooooooooooooooooooooaaaaaaaaaaaaaaaaaaaaaallllllllllllllllllllllllllllllllllllll!!!!!!!!!!!!!!!!!!!!!

Leo wasn't thinking about saving energy now. He ran off to celebrate with his arms raised in the air.

But France weren't going to give up either. They equalised with their second penalty of the match, and Leo felt a sinking feeling again. What would it take to win this final?!

After all that exhausting drama, Leo had to prepare himself for the penalty shoot-out. He took a deep breath. He was sure it had been a great final for everyone watching at home, but it was so stressful on the pitch.

'I'll take the first one,' he said without hesitation. Once again, he saw it as his job to show his teammates the way.

He had already taken a penalty against the France

keeper during the match, so he had a decision to make. Should he stick with focusing on the same side, or aim for the other corner this time? What would the keeper be expecting?

Leo decided to go to the opposite side. He strolled forward, watching the keeper closely, and then calmly side-footed the ball into that corner. Yes!

When France dragged a penalty wide, Argentina had the advantage. As teammate Gonzalo Montiel was preparing to take the winning kick, Leo could hardly watch.

While they waited, every second felt like an hour. Then Montiel fired the ball into the net.

Leo fell to his knees and raised his arms towards the sky. His teammates swarmed around him, with hugs and tears. Argentina had done it! Leo's World Cup dream had come true at last.

'I'm so happy for you!' Coach Scaloni said, celebrating with his star man. 'No one deserves this moment more than you.'

Leo hurried over to the Argentina fans, waving and smiling. None of them seemed to be leaving any time soon. They had been through all the ups and downs with him at major tournaments, and they had been fantastic here in Qatar. It was great to see the joy on their faces.

As captain, Leo would have the special job of lifting the trophy. He could feel his legs shaking, a combination of exhaustion and the overwhelming emotions running through his body. Just like on the pitch, he marked the moment in style, carrying the famous golden trophy slowly towards his teammates and savouring the suspense before raising it to the sky.

In front of the microphone, just minutes after winning the World Cup, Leo was in a happy daze. A million thoughts were rushing through his head. How was he meant to summarise this whole journey with Argentina in a few sentences?!

Football fans would probably never agree on the debate of whether Leo was the GOAT, but how could he not be after these World Cup heroics? While the celebrations continued in the dressing room, he smiled with the happiness of a man who had just checked off one of the last big dreams of his career .

CHAPTER 15

KYLIAN MBAPPÉ, 2022 WORLD CUP

Savouring the spotlight

If you have just read the Lionel Messi chapter, you will already know the ending to Kylian Mbappé's 2022 World Cup final experience. But that doesn't tell the whole story – because before that crushing shoot-out experience of loss for France, Kylian had lit up another tournament and added to his World Cup highlight reel.

Those highlights had begun with Kylian's dramatic rise as a teenager at the 2018 World Cup. It was one of those iconic tournament performances, and he had dazzled the football world with four goals and some blistering runs. Everyone agreed that they were watching a future superstar.

Was it fair to expect the same highlights again in 2022? Maybe not, but Kylian usually found a way to hit a higher level in the biggest games.

A lot had changed for him since the last tournament. He had settled into a starring role for Paris Saint-Germain and so was now teammates with Messi and Neymar. In this current French squad, he wasn't the young wildcard anymore. He was the main man.

Kylian demonstrated that by taking over in Qatar with some unstoppable performances. He scored against Australia in the first group game, then smashed a double to beat Denmark. There was really nothing more terrifying for a defender than being left one-on-one against Kylian with lots of space behind.

'Look for the through ball,' Kylian told his teammates. 'If there's a race for the ball, I'm going to win it.'

Against Poland in the second round, it was 'The Kylian Show'. The warning signs were there in the first half when he left a defender on the ground and fired a shot into the side-netting, but the Poland defence still gave him too much space just before half-time and he set up Olivier Giroud for a 1–0 lead.

'Don't they know they should be marking you?!' Olivier asked with a grin as they celebrated together in front of the French fans.

Then it was Kylian's turn in the spotlight. He was unmarked as France counterattacked, and he smashed a shot into the top corner.

Goooooooooooooooooooooooaaaaaaaaaaaaaaaaaaaaaaallllllllllllllllllllllllllllllllll!!!!!!!!!!!!!!!!!!!!!!

He turned to the fans with a look that said: 'That's just what I do.'

Kylian would celebrate again in that same corner of the stadium in stoppage time, after whipping another stunner past the Poland keeper.

Goooooooooooooooooooooooaaaaaaaaaaaaaaaaaaaaaaallllllllllllllllllllllllllllllllll!!!!!!!!!!!!!!!!!!!!!!

With his trademark arms-folded brand of celebration, Kylian was leading his team into the next round.

France edged past England in their quarter-final,

before ending Morocco's fairytale run in the semis. Kylian and his teammates had been here before in big tournaments, and those experiences definitely helped.

In 2018, Kylian had scored one of France's four goals in the World Cup final. Now in 2022, he was heading back to the final once again, and this French squad wasn't going to give up the trophy without a fight.

A mountain to climb

As Kylian stepped into the tunnel, he felt nervous on the inside. He was still only 23 years old, and he knew the whole world would be watching today. But on the outside, he played it cool. He winked at the camera and smiled at the mascot who would be walking next to him.

His smile didn't last long, though. Before France could settle into the game, Argentina were in complete control, winning every 50-50 ball and racing into a 2–0 lead. The stadium was rocking, and all the noise was coming from the Argentina fans.

France boss Didier Deschamps was pacing on the touchline, and Kylian had a stunned look on his face. None of this was how they had pictured the final.

When the referee blew his whistle for half time, Kylian puffed out his cheeks. He hadn't given up hope, but he knew France had a mountain to climb in the second half.

In the dressing room, they had 15 minutes to clear their heads and refocus. That wasn't much time to make tactical changes, but it was enough of a pause to help remember what made the team so strong.

'Look, it only takes one goal to put the pressure back on Argentina,' Didier explained. 'Crazy things can happen in finals, and there's a long way to go.'

'Don't rush things,' Kylian added, standing up and looking at his teammates. 'We can find gaps in their defence, and I'll be there to do the rest.'

The France players returned to the pitch with renewed confidence. With the talent in their team, they truly believed that the final was far from over.

Leading the comeback

France battled back, but they struggled to create chances. Argentina were happy to let the seconds creep by, and they still looked like a threat to score a third goal. Kylian tried not to glance up at the clock on the scoreboard, but he had to check. He gulped. Less than 15 minutes to go. If there was going to be a miracle, it had to happen now.

Kylian reached a long pass and prodded it over the top of the defence for Randal Kolo Muani to chase. Kolo Muani sped clear, but then he was pulled down in the box.

Penalty! Kylian had his arms raised in the air before the referee even made his decision. Out of nothing, France had a route back into the game. Kylian arrowed the penalty towards the bottom corner and let out a shout as it squeezed past the keeper's dive.

Goooooooooooooooooooooooaaaaaaaaaaaaaaaaaa aaaaallllllllllllllllllllllllllllllllllll!!!!!!!!!!!!!!!!!!!!!!

'Come on!!!' he yelled, pumping his fist and sprinting to get the ball out of the net. 'We're still in this!'

France were everywhere now. A minute later, they muscled Messi off the ball, then attacked again. Kylian cushioned a header to substitute Marcus Thuram and yelled for the one-two. Marcus lifted the ball back to him, and Kylian decided: 'Why not?'

He would have to take the shot on the volley before an Argentina defender could stretch for a block, and Kylian watched the ball like a hawk before sweeping a shot across the keeper. He struck it perfectly, right off the laces, and it whizzed into the bottom corner.

Gooooooooooooooooooooooaaaaaaaaaaaaaaaaa aaaaalllllllllllllllllllllllllllllllllll!!!!!!!!!!!!!!!!!!!!!!!!

'He is an awesome force of nature!' the commentator roared.

What a feeling! Kylian ran towards the fans with his arms outstretched. A player like him could never be counted out.

The adrenaline was still soaring for Kylian as the game went into extra time, but his heart sank when Argentina retook the lead. Once again, France were racing against the clock.

A corner reached Kylian at the edge of the box. As

he controlled the ball, his only thought was to unleash a quick shot. But an Argentina arm blocked it from testing the keeper – and the defender was in the box! The referee pointed to the spot for the third time.

This was already among the most dramatic World Cup finals ever, and Kylian now had another chance to save France. He chose where he wanted to place the penalty and beat the Argentina keeper again.

Gooooooooooooooooooooooaaaaaaaaaaaaaaaaa aaaaalllllllllllllllllllllllllllllllllll!!!!!!!!!!!!!!!!!!!!!

A World Cup final hat-trick! Kylian could barely believe it himself. It was as if he had stepped outside of his body for the last few hours.

The showdown between Kylian and his friend Messi had lived up to all the pre-game hype. Neither of them deserved to be on the losing team, but unfortunately there could only be one winner.

Penalty pain

There was no way to separate two brilliant teams, so it came down to the dreaded penalty shoot-out. In some ways, it felt like a shame after all the end-to-end action. It also sent Kylian back to the penalty spot for the third time in the last hour. There was just time to catch his breath and scoop up a water bottle before he had the ball back in his hands.

His golden boots hadn't let him down so far, and he confidently fired his penalty past the keeper's dive. With relief all over his face, Kylian looked over to the France fans with a fist pump and signalled for them to get louder.

As he walked back to the halfway line, Kylian knew his job was done. Now he could only watch helplessly as his teammates stepped forward for the most high-pressure penalties imaginable.

Then came the shoot-out pain. France put a penalty just wide, and Argentina slotted home the winning kick. It had been an unforgettable night of football, but this time, Kylian had to accept being on the losing side.

He tried to compose himself to get his runners-up medal and collect the Golden Boot award for his eight tournament goals. But it was a lonely place to be for the French players. They stared into the distance and digested what had happened, while the Argentina celebrations continued just a few metres away.

When enough time had passed, Kylian was able to look back on the tournament. He wished that France had found a way to finish off their famous fightback, but he had no other regrets. He had given everything – they all had – and he was determined to come back even stronger for the next World Cup in 2026.

TEST YOUR KNOWLEDGE

QUESTIONS

1. Which player scored two headers to win the 1998 World Cup final?

2. Which two players scored hat-tricks in the World Cup final?

3. How many goals did Brazil's Ronaldo score during the 2002 World Cup tournament?

4. Against which team did Harry Kane net a hat-trick at the 2018 World Cup?

5. True or False: Diego Maradona scored two goals against England at the 1986 World Cup.

6. Italy captain Fabio Cannavaro took over the captain's armband from which legendary defender?

7. Andrés Iniesta scored the 2010 World Cup-winning goal in the final against which team?

8. How many saves did Tim Howard make in his record-setting World Cup performance?

9. Lionel Messi scored two of Argentina's goals in the 2022 World Cup final – but who scored the other goal?

10. True or False: Pelé was just 19 years old at the 1970 World Cup.

11. At the 1974 World Cup, who were the Netherlands' opponents when Johan Cruyff first performed his 'Cruyff Turn'?

1. *Zinedine Zidane* **2.** *Geoff Hurst and Kylian Mbappé* **3.** *Eight* **4.** *Panama* **5.** *True* **6.** *Paolo Maldini* **7.** *The Netherlands* **8.** *Sixteen* **9.** *Ángel Di María* **10.** *False (he was twenty-nine)* **11.** *Sweden*

HOW THE WORLD CUP 2026 WILL WORK

From 2026, the World Cup tournament structure will be different from previous ones! The amount of teams competing has increased from 32 to 48, so there will be even more countries competing in the World Cup than ever before. To make room for the extra teams, group stages will consist of 12 groups of four teams, up from eight groups previously.

In these group stages, each team will play three matches. Once these matches are complete, the two top teams from each group advance. But in addition to this, the eight best third-placed teams will advance too, leading to the new first round of knockouts: The round of 32. After this, it goes to the regular Round of 16, Quarter-Finals, Semi-Finals and then the Final!

This means there will be more matches, more countries, and even more action to make this the biggest World Cup tournament of all time!

TOURNAMENT PLANNER

It's finally here, the 2026 World Cup Tournament! Fill in the tables over the page when all the group games have been played, then continue with the round of 32, round of 16, Quarter-Final and Semi-Finals to plot the path all the way to the Final!

P	=	Played
W	=	Won
D	=	Drawn
L	=	Lost
F	=	Goals for
A	=	Goals against
PTS	=	Points

GROUP STAGE

GROUP A	P	W	D	L	F	A	PTS
Mexico							
South Africa							
Korea Republic							
CZE/DEN/ IRL/MKD							

GROUP B	P	W	D	L	F	A	PTS
Canada							
BIH/ITA/NIR/ WAL							
Quatar							
Switzerland							

GROUP C	P	W	D	L	F	A	PTS
Brazil							
Morroco							
Haiti							
Scotland							

GROUP D	P	W	D	L	F	A	PTS
USA							
Paraguay							
Australia							
KOS/ROU/ SVK/TUR							

GROUP E	P	W	D	L	F	A	PTS
Germany							
Curaçao							
Côte D'Ivoire							
Ecuador							

GROUP F	P	W	D	L	F	A	PTS
Netherlands							
Japan							
ALB/POL/ SWE/UKR							
Tunisia							

GROUP G	P	W	D	L	F	A	PTS
Belgium							
Egypt							
IR Iran							
New Zealand							

GROUP H	P	W	D	L	F	A	PTS
Spain							
Cabo Verde							
Saudi Arabia							
Uruguay							

GROUP I	P	W	D	L	F	A	PTS
France							
Senegal							
BOL/IRQ/SUR							
Norway							

GROUP J	P	W	D	L	F	A	PTS
Argentina							
Algeria							
Austria							
Jordan							

GROUP K	P	W	D	L	F	A	PTS
Portugal							
COD/JAM/ NCL							
Uzbekistan							
Columbia							

GROUP L	P	W	D	L	F	A	PTS
England							
Croatia							
Ghana							
Panama							

ROUND OF 32

The winner and the runner-up of each group go through to the Round of 32, plus four of the best-performing third placed teams. Fill in the teams and the scores below.

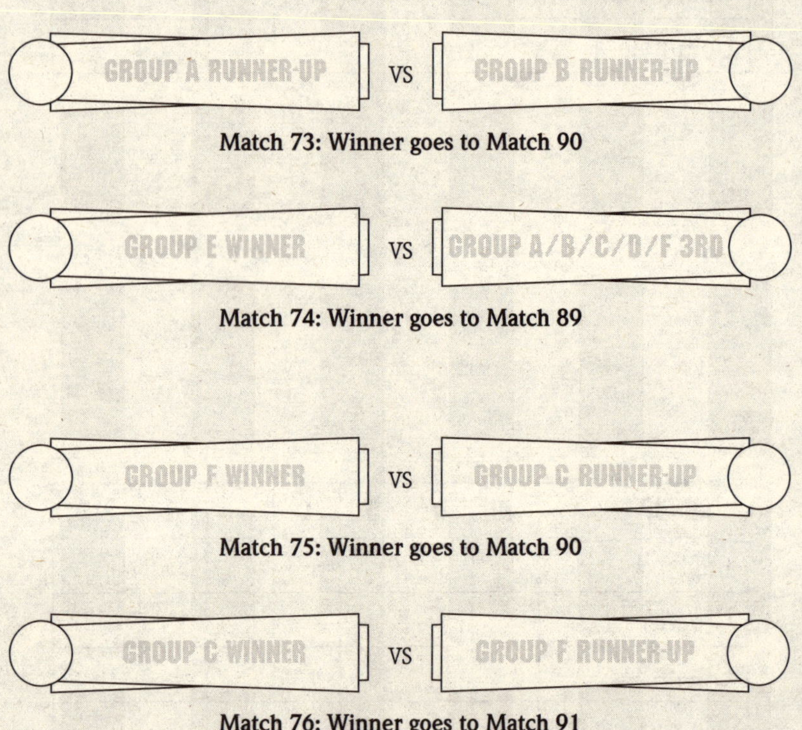

Match 73: Winner goes to Match 90

Match 74: Winner goes to Match 89

Match 75: Winner goes to Match 90

Match 76: Winner goes to Match 91

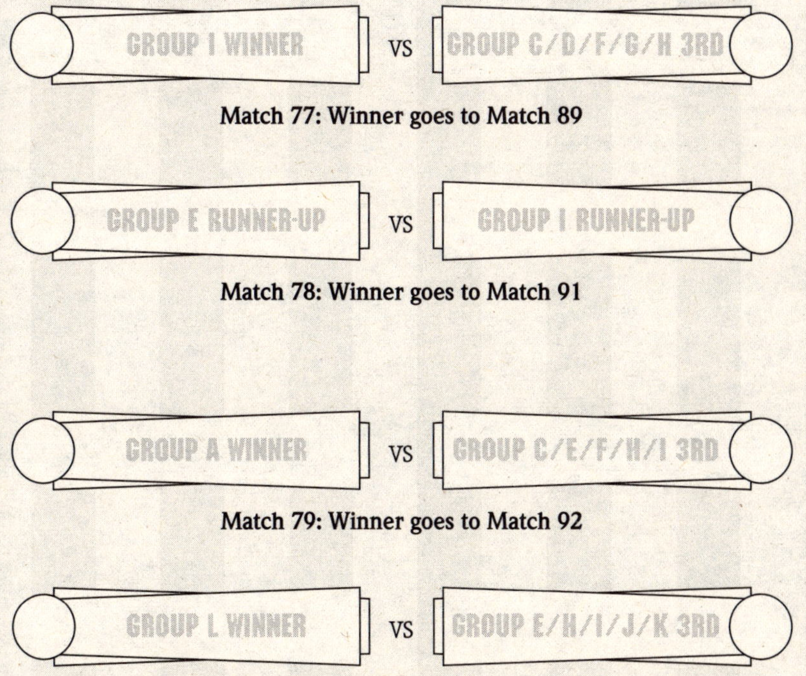

Match 77: Winner goes to Match 89

Match 78: Winner goes to Match 91

Match 79: Winner goes to Match 92

Match 80: Winner goes to Match 92

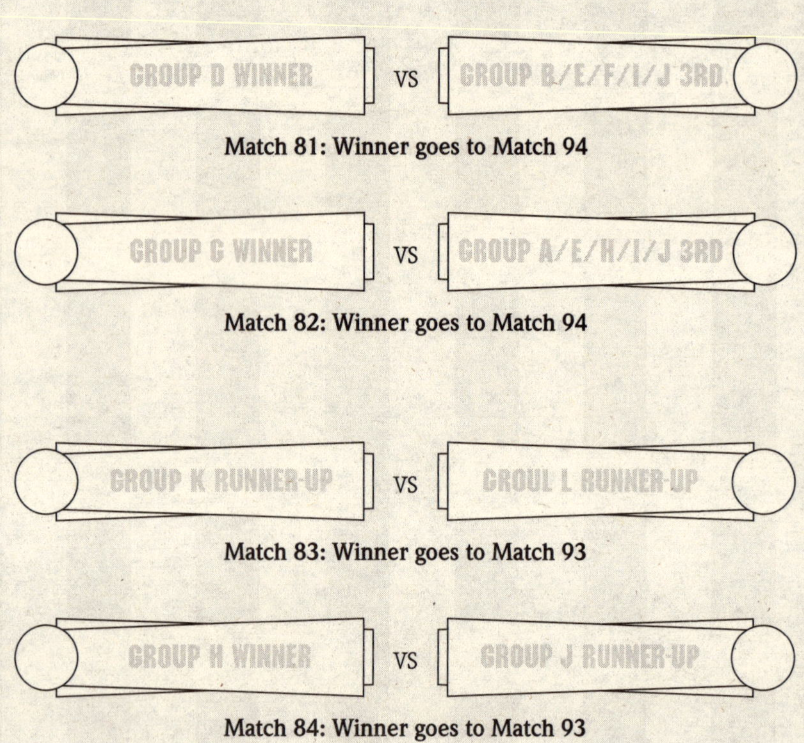

Match 81: Winner goes to Match 94

Match 82: Winner goes to Match 94

Match 83: Winner goes to Match 93

Match 84: Winner goes to Match 93

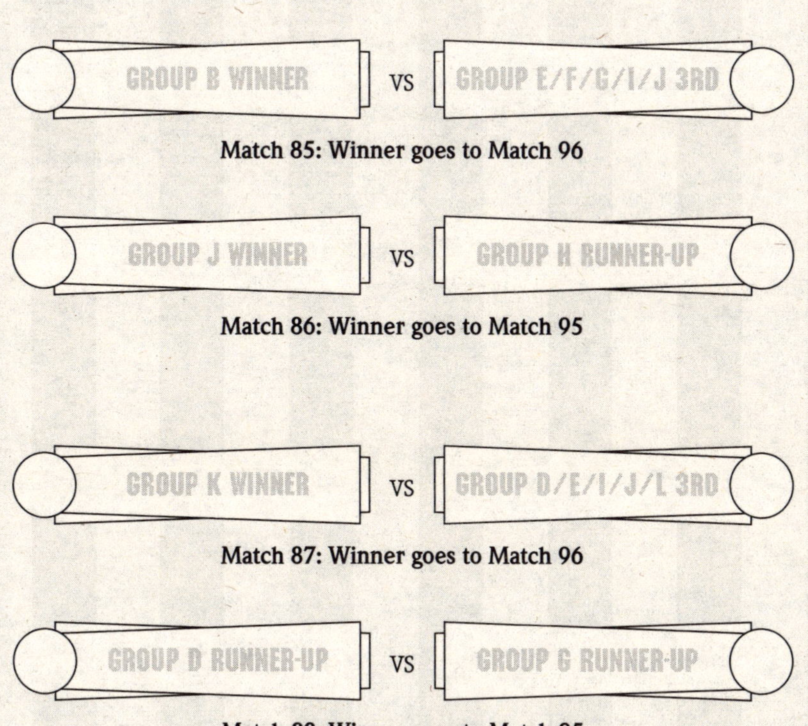

Match 85: Winner goes to Match 96

Match 86: Winner goes to Match 95

Match 87: Winner goes to Match 96

Match 88: Winner goes to Match 95

LAST 16

The winner and the runner-up of each group go through to the Round of 16, plus four of the best-performing third placed teams. Fill in the teams and the scores below.

MATCH 74 WINNER vs MATCH 77 WINNER

Match 89: Winner goes to Match 97

MATCH 73 WINNER vs MATCH 75 WINNER

Match 90: Winner goes to Match 97

MATCH 76 WINNER vs MATCH 78 WINNER

Match 91: Winner goes to Match 99

MATCH 79 WINNER vs MATCH 80 WINNER

Match 92: Winner goes to Match 99

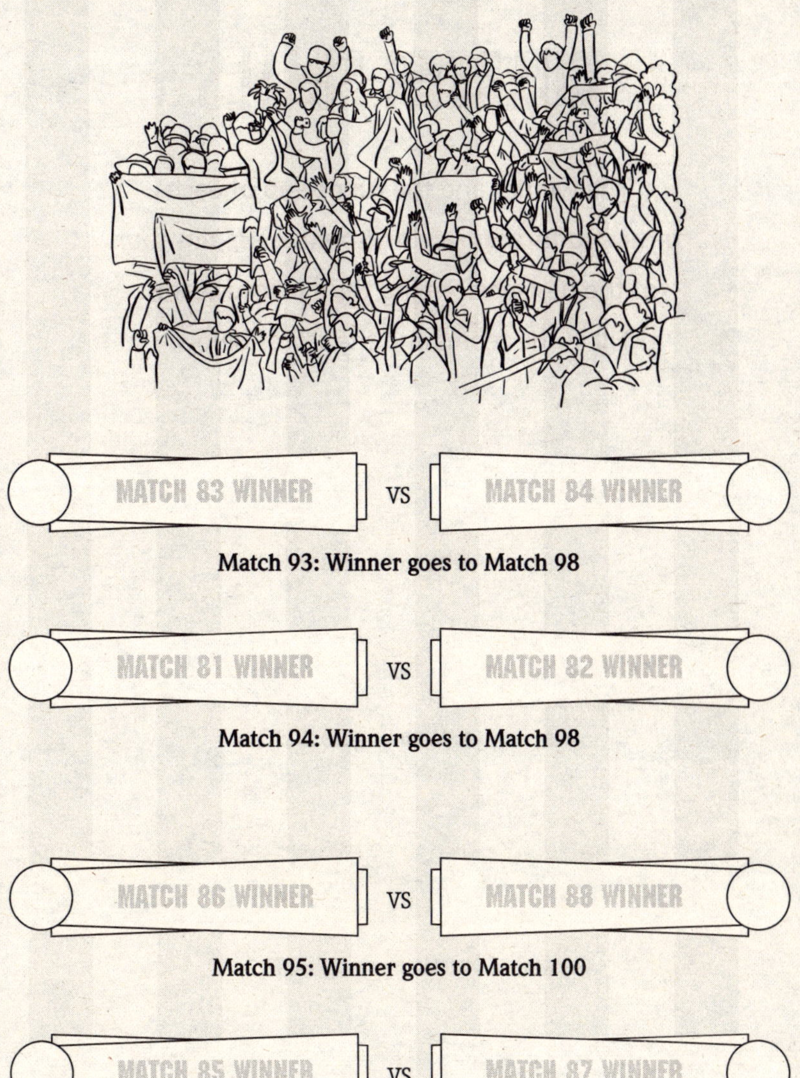

MATCH 83 WINNER vs MATCH 84 WINNER

Match 93: Winner goes to Match 98

MATCH 81 WINNER vs MATCH 82 WINNER

Match 94: Winner goes to Match 98

MATCH 86 WINNER vs MATCH 88 WINNER

Match 95: Winner goes to Match 100

MATCH 85 WINNER vs MATCH 87 WINNER

Match 96: Winner goes to Match 100

QUARTER FINALS

The winner and the runner-up of each group go through to the Round of 8, plus four of the best-performing third placed teams. Fill in the teams and the scores below.

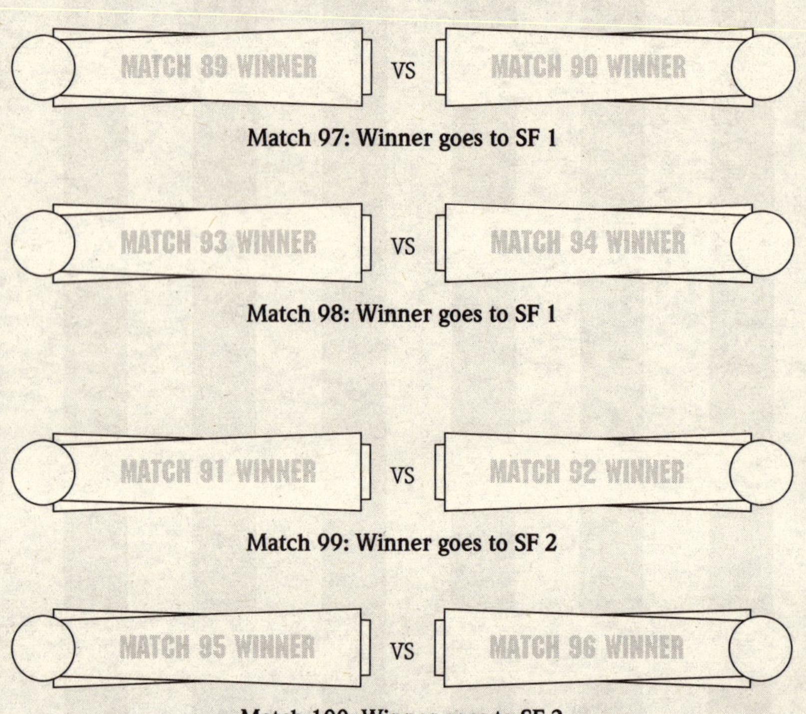

SEMI FINALS

Nearly there – the winners of these go to the finals, the loser to the third place match.

SF 1 · **Winner goes to Final**

QF 1 WINNER vs QF 2 WINNER

SF 2 · **Winner goes to Final**

QF 3 WINNER vs QF 4 WINNER

THE 2026 WORLD CUP FINAL

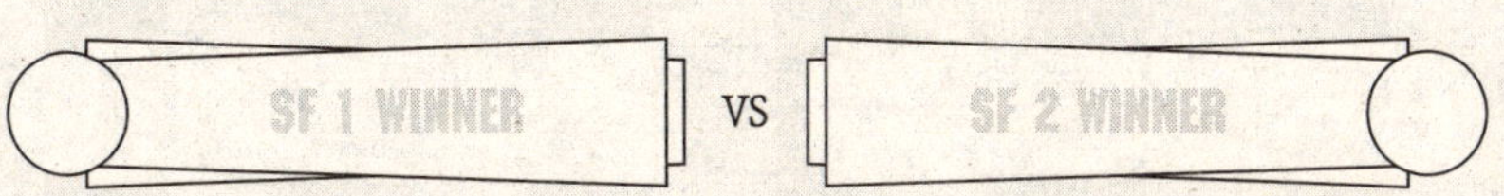

TOURNAMENT SUMMARY CHART

When it's all over, you can fill in all the details. How did your team do? Did you support a World Cup-winning team, or is it a case of better luck next time?

Winner __________

Runner-up __________

Third place __________

Fourth place __________

Golden boot __________

Goal of the tournament scored by __________

Best match __________

Number of goals scored __________

Number of yellow cards __________

Number of red cards __________

DRAW YOUR OWN BADGE

Use the space below to design your very own badge – think about how it will look when it is small on a shirt – and colour it in when you are done. Use family or football imagery, or things that relate to the city or countryside around you to make it look really special.

DESIGN YOUR OWN KIT

Now, here is your chance to make up your very own international kit! This could be a special edition for your school team, the team you support, or your family football team. Use the space below to draw in the details. You can have advertising if you like, to make it look really professional!

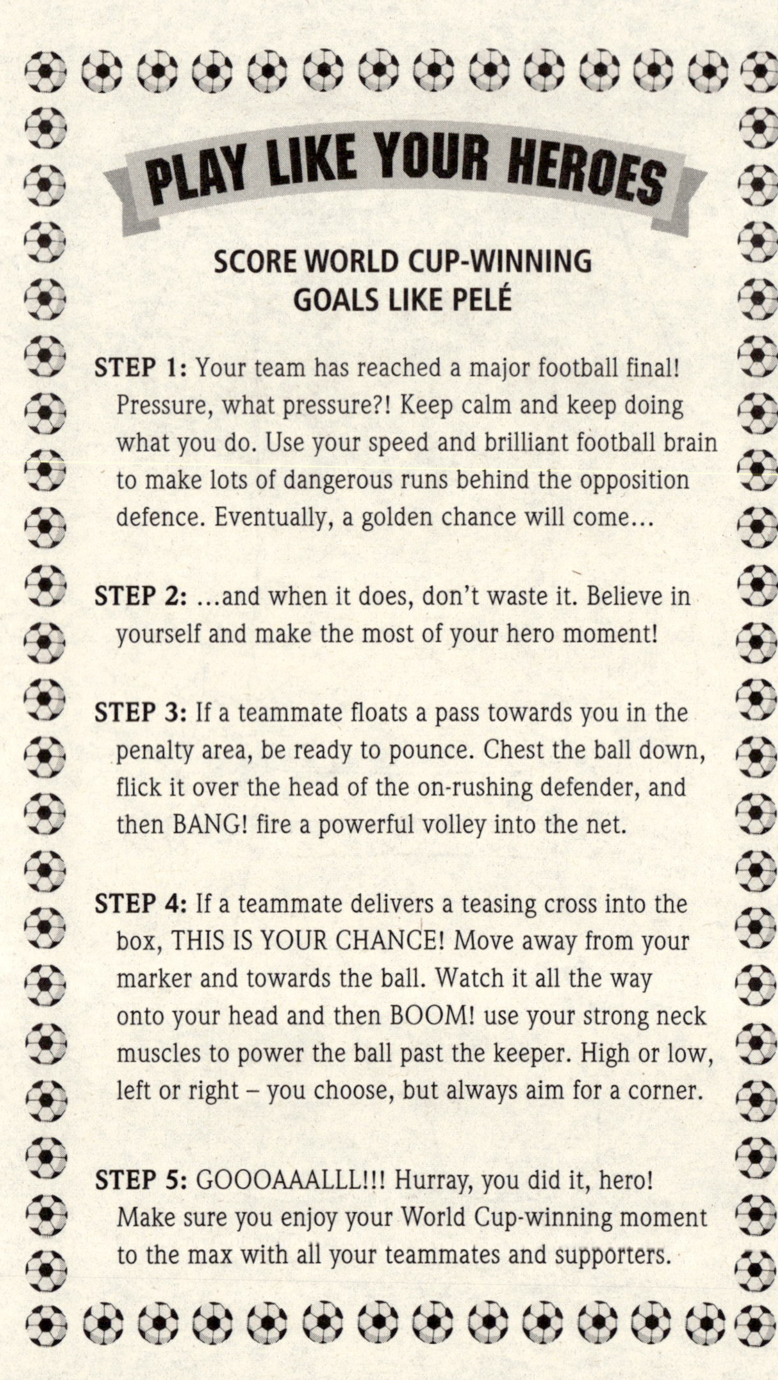

PLAY LIKE YOUR HEROES

SCORE WORLD CUP-WINNING GOALS LIKE PELÉ

STEP 1: Your team has reached a major football final! Pressure, what pressure?! Keep calm and keep doing what you do. Use your speed and brilliant football brain to make lots of dangerous runs behind the opposition defence. Eventually, a golden chance will come...

STEP 2: ...and when it does, don't waste it. Believe in yourself and make the most of your hero moment!

STEP 3: If a teammate floats a pass towards you in the penalty area, be ready to pounce. Chest the ball down, flick it over the head of the on-rushing defender, and then BANG! fire a powerful volley into the net.

STEP 4: If a teammate delivers a teasing cross into the box, THIS IS YOUR CHANCE! Move away from your marker and towards the ball. Watch it all the way onto your head and then BOOM! use your strong neck muscles to power the ball past the keeper. High or low, left or right – you choose, but always aim for a corner.

STEP 5: GOOOAAALLL!!! Hurray, you did it, hero! Make sure you enjoy your World Cup-winning moment to the max with all your teammates and supporters.

18 **THE FACTS**

NAME: Pelé, or Edson Arantes Do Nascimento

DATE OF BIRTH: 23 October 1940

AGE: Died in 2022, aged 82

PLACE OF BIRTH: Três Corações

NATIONALITY: Brazilian

CLUBS: Santos, New York Cosmos

POSITION: ST

THE STATS	
Height (cm):	173
Club appearances:	1363
Club goals:	1281
Club trophies:	26
International appearances:	92
International goals:	77
International trophies:	3
Ballon d'Ors:	1

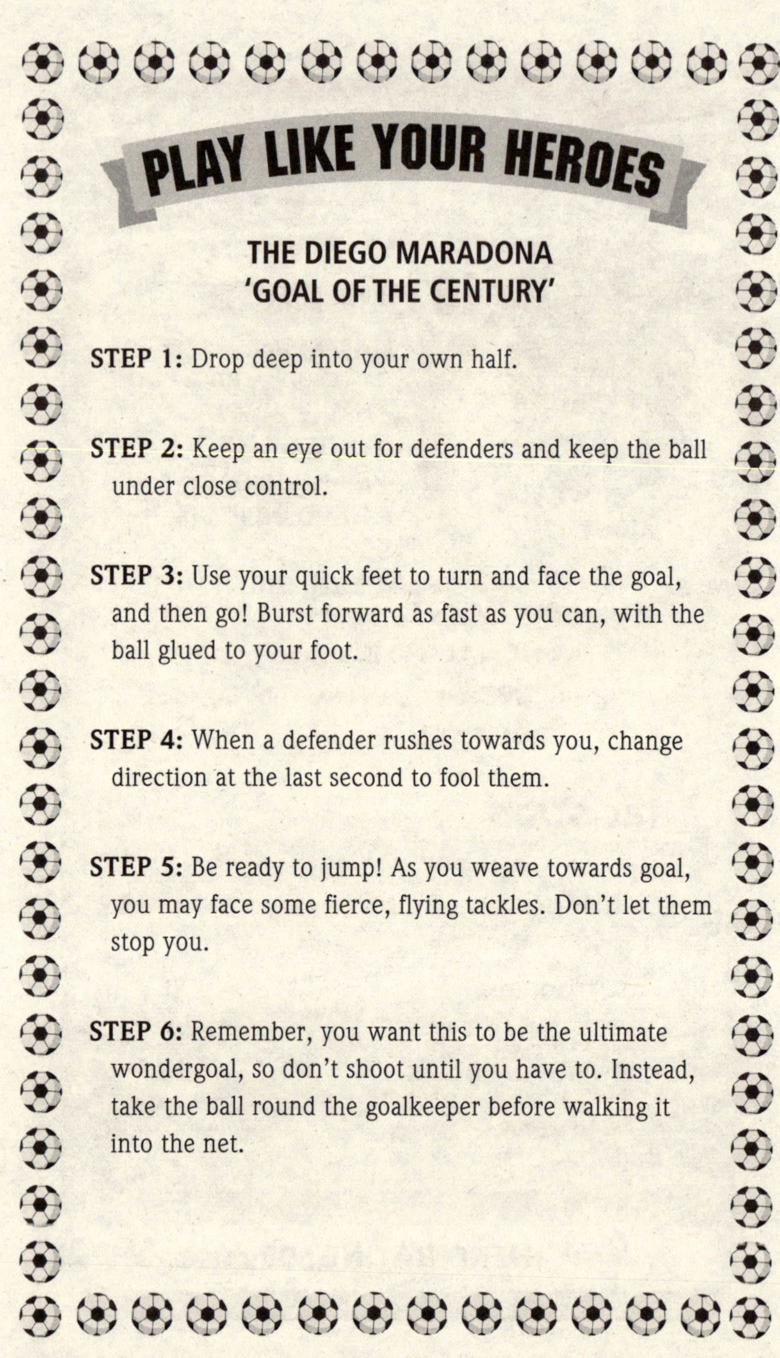

PLAY LIKE YOUR HEROES

THE DIEGO MARADONA 'GOAL OF THE CENTURY'

STEP 1: Drop deep into your own half.

STEP 2: Keep an eye out for defenders and keep the ball under close control.

STEP 3: Use your quick feet to turn and face the goal, and then go! Burst forward as fast as you can, with the ball glued to your foot.

STEP 4: When a defender rushes towards you, change direction at the last second to fool them.

STEP 5: Be ready to jump! As you weave towards goal, you may face some fierce, flying tackles. Don't let them stop you.

STEP 6: Remember, you want this to be the ultimate wondergoal, so don't shoot until you have to. Instead, take the ball round the goalkeeper before walking it into the net.

MARADONA

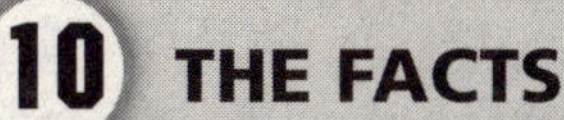

10 THE FACTS

NAME: Diego Armando Maradona Franco

DATE OF BIRTH: 30 October 1960

PLACE OF BIRTH: Buenos Aires

NATIONALITY: Argentinian

BEST FRIEND: Claudio Caniggia

MAIN CLUB: Boca Juniors, Barcelona and Napoli

POSITION: RW

THE STATS

Height (cm):	**165**
Club appearances:	**590**
Club goals:	**312**
Club assists:	**59**
Club trophies:	**9**
International appearances:	**91**
International goals:	**34**
International trophies:	**1**
Ballon d'Ors:	**1**

★★★ **HERO RATING: 95** ★★★

CAN'T GET ENOUGH OF

ULTIMATE FOOTBALL HEROES?

Check out heroesfootball.com for quizzes, games, and competitions!

Plus join the Ultimate Football Heroes Fan Club to score exclusive content and be the first to hear about new books and events.

heroesfootball.com/subscribe/